Critical Acclaim for the Previous Edition

"A splendid book." —*The Fresno Bee*

". . . this handbook for prospective and current stepfamilies provides solid suggestions and comforting support. Both the psychological and the practical aspects of the creation of a new family . . . are thoroughly discussed, as are the many complex relationships that result. Relationships old and new are explored in all their permutations, with telling examples and sensible advice. . . . This is a welcome resource." —*The Kirkus Reviews*

". . . a guide with humor and wisdom discussing divorce, single parenting, communicating with former spouses, helping children adjust, discipline, even legal issues. . . . This book can provide good insight." —*Practical Parenting*

"The Vishers . . . offer a constructive strategy for building a strong family unit after remarriage. . . . Their matter-of-fact, seasoned advice will be useful for laypersons coping with ready-made families." —*The Library Journal*

". . . clearly written, optimistic, and practical . . . useful to stepfamilies. . . . This book is an important one for the reconstituted family, its members, as well as professionals working in the field. It is all the more important because of the lack of other books and publications to deal with these issues. As such, it would be very much appreciated by the public at large." —CHRISSOULA STAVRAKAKI, M.D. *Psychiatry Journal of the University of Ottawa*

"Provide[s] a confident approach to confronting the difficulties encountered by stepparents and children alike as they struggle to achieve satisfying family lives. The book's optimistic tone contrasts sharply with the gloom which so often permeates the literature on divorce and families. . . . Makes a significant contribution." —JEAN GOLDSMITH, PH.D. Northeastern University Medical School

HOW TO WIN AS A STEPFAMILY

Second Edition

Emily B. Visher, Ph.D.
and
John S. Visher, M.D.

BRUNNER/MAZEL, *Publishers* • NEW YORK

Library of Congress Cataloging-in-Publication Data
Visher, Emily B.
    How to win as a stepfamily / by Emily B. Visher and John S.
Visher.—2nd ed.
        p. cm.
    Reprint. Originally published: New York : Dembner Books, 1982.
    Includes bibliographical references and index.
    ISBN 0-87630-649-0
    1. Stepfamilies—United States.   2. Stepparents—United States.
3. Stepchildren—United States.   I. Visher, John S.
II. Title.
HQ777.7.V56   1991
306.874—dc20   91-23000
                                                                    CIP

Published by
BRUNNER/MAZEL, INC.
19 Union Square West
New York, New York 10003

Manufactured in the United States of America

10 9 8 7 6 5 4 3 2

To the many stepfamilies
who have shared with us
their disappointments and frustrations
and also the warmth and joy
of their loving and caring.

Contents

Introduction

Our stepfamily adventure began in 1959 when we promised to love one another and care for the assortment of children who stood close behind us—eight in all, ranging in age from five to 15 years.

Since we were both in the mental health field, we made the assumption that our knowledge of emotions and behavior would carry us through any difficult spots we might encounter. *That was our first mistake!*

We looked for a book or two on stepfamily life (without success), sought therapeutic assistance from time to time, and muddled along— creating our own roles and rules as we progressed.

Then, ever so slowly, we began to realize that we were being unrealistic in our expectations. We also recognized that we were meeting an ever increasing number of people who were joining families with the same lack of forethought and unrealistic expectations we had clung to for so long.

By 1975 half a million new stepfamilies were being created every year in the United States, and our personal interest combined with our professional concern for the complex families that came to us for help. The bells started ringing in our heads and we began to try to learn all we could about this type of family.

Since then, we have learned much—from our children, from our friends and colleagues, from the stepfamilies we meet and those we work with, and from our involvement with Stepfamily Association of California and then with Stepfamily Association of America.

There is much more to learn, but the past years have shown some directions and paths to follow. Stepfamilies have shared with us their fears and concerns, their joys and their sorrows, their successes and failures. Guidelines have emerged from research in this area. Personally, although we still run into rough spots, as all families do, we are deeply grateful for the added richness and number of close relationships we have experienced as a result of the complexity of our stepfamily structure. Professionally, we keep listening and learning and doing what we can to clarify the realities of this type of family for the individuals in stepfamilies, and for the communities in which stepfamilies live.

This book contains information and specific suggestions for the adults involved in making their stepfamilies work. For illustration we have included many personal anecdotes. There are challenges in all types of families, and success in meeting these challenges brings a sense of personal strength and mastery. We hope this book will be a helpful guide for dealing with the specific challenges of the stepfamily.

Stepfamilies can be good families in which to raise children. They can be good families in which to find personal satisfaction and growth. They can be good families in which to develop close emotional adult relationships.

We hold a deep conviction that with information and support remarried parents and stepparents can utilize their individual strengths to create families which will provide an atmosphere favorable to growth and development and rich in deep emotional rewards.

Emily and John Visher

Lafayette, California

HOW TO WIN AS A STEPFAMILY

Second Edition

1 | Stepfamilies Look in the Mirror

When stepfamilies look in the mirror, what do they see? They see that being a stepparent is different from being a parent, that being a remarried parent is different from being a parent in a first marriage, and that growing up in a stepfamily can be even more complicated than growing up with only one set of parents. And it all looks hazy and confusing.

The raising of children is not easy in any family, but for stepparents it is doubly difficult. Because of the complicated nature of stepfamilies, numerous challenges and questions arise which are not talked about in the thousands of books written about child-rearing. There is no Dr. Spock for stepparents and remarried parents.

When we speak of stepfamilies, we mean families in which there is an adult couple in the household with at least one of the adults having a child by a previous marriage. Some couples are married; others are not. In some stepfamilies only one parent has children, while in others both adults have children. The number of different custody and visitation arrangements is mind boggling! But even though there are a tremendous number of family patterns, we have found there are common characteristics in "recoupled" families with children from a former marriage that produce many similar feelings and raise many similar questions. That is why we used the term "stepfamily" to refer to all of them.

If you are a stepchild or a stepparent, you may feel as though you are stumbling along an unfamiliar path in partial or total darkness, and although there are millions of other American adults who are stepparents, the path sometimes looks and feels absolutely deserted. You don't even know if there are rocks in the way or traps around the next corner.

Since adults and children in any type of family have similar goals, it seems to many people that the path for recoupled families is the same as for a first marriage family. The two adults will join together to support each other and to help the children on their way. However, when difficulties arise, for many remarried adults an alarm goes off in their heads warning, "You're doing it again. You can't manage a family—there's something really wrong with you!" The insecurity and anxiety rush in and the whole venture seems frightening and frustrating. It's hard to believe that you're not the cause of all the upset.

Even though people react to situations in their own particular ways, the stepfamily journey has many special turnings which you need to learn about and consider. It is a complicated journey because many more people are involved in many more complicated relationships than in first marriage families and there are important characteristics that set stepfamilies apart from other families.* We believe that many of the stresses and strains that pull at stepfamilies can be handled with much greater ease if you know what these characteristics are and how they may affect your particular family.

---

*Some differences between stepfamilies and nuclear families are indicated in table form in Appendix A.

There have been many losses

Marge came to see a counselor because she was crying a lot and didn't know why. She thought there must be something terribly wrong with her. She had been married to Lawrence for four months and had moved from another city with her nine-year-old son, Mark, to be with Lawrence and his ten-year-old twins, Les and Len. Previously, Marge had been married for seven years and divorced for two years. During the past five years she had worked as the manager of a small office, receiving a great deal of praise for her management skills. As for her son Mark, after school he had stayed with his grandparents until Marge was free to pick him up on her way home from work.

Now that they had joined their children in one family, Marge and Lawrence felt that it was important for Marge to be home to see to the needs of the three children. The new stepfamily, however, was not working smoothly. Many important losses had gone unrecognized so that the individuals were feeling emotionally drained and unhappy. Marge and her children had experienced the losses that go along with geographic change and the leaving of old friends and associates. In addition, Marge had given up a job which gave her much personal satisfaction and support, in exchange for a homemaker's assignment where she missed the stimulation of other adults. Instead, she was eyed with suspicion as an intruder by Lawrence's children and regarded as a deserter by her own son, who was now one person in a household of five rather than the only child in a household of two. Lawrence felt as though he was continually giving and not receiving in return as he struggled to keep Les and Len under control, while at the same time trying to deal with his wife's unhappiness. In addition, Mark missed his grandparents.

Once Marge and Lawrence realized they all were dealing with important losses, they looked for ways to bring more satisfactions into their lives. That way there would be energy and support coming in as well as going out. Marge found a position suited to her managerial talents and once again had working days filled with personal interest and adult appreciation. Mark and his grandparents saw each other more frequently. Gradually, new relationships within the household became less forced and emotionally demanding. Gains slowly replaced the losses, and the household members no longer felt as though their inner reservoirs had run dry.

You, too, may find yourself feeling depressed or on the verge of crying at times when nothing seems to be going right or when the children are dragging around with unhappy faces and spending most of their time closeted alone in their rooms. It is helpful to be aware that these feelings and behaviors often occur because in stepfamilies adults and children have all experienced important losses in their lives.

It is true that there are changes, and therefore losses, in first marriages. You may have moved to a new city, or changed jobs, or left your parents' home. However, the losses experienced by all the people involved in a remarriage, children as well as adults, involve not only changes similar to those just mentioned, but also many more deeply felt losses that have been overlooked or considered unimportant or forgotten because they occurred some months or years before. For example, you may have experienced:

- loss of a relationship with a husband or wife because of a death or divorce. This is a loss even when the divorce was desired.
- loss of the dreams and expectations of what your first marriage would be like.
- loss of a daily parent-child relationship.
- loss of support from family and friends.
- loss of a familiar community, school, job.
- loss of a familiar role in the family.

Because you are happy with your new relationship, it may seem as though there is something wrong with you if you also have sad feelings. But sadness is there, too, just as it was when you graduated from school and were excited to be finished and getting a job, yet also sad at the loss of friends and familiar activities and surroundings.

There may also be sadness that your previous marriage did not work out, or that you do not live with your children all the time anymore, or that this first marriage for you is not the first marriage for your spouse, so that you are relating to partly grown children and to someone who is an ex-spouse.

Subsequent families are structurally and emotionally different from first families. Upset and sadness are experienced by the children and at times by the adults as they react to the loss of their biological family or to the loss of a dream of a perfect marriage. Acceptance that a stepfamily is a different type of family is important, as is the recognition that many upsetting behaviors result from these feelings of insecurity and loss.

It may be difficult to share these feelings with your partner because it seems to one or both of you that if you really are in love there should be no sadness of this kind. Such reactions, however, may be related to situations like those mentioned, rather than to the relationship between the two of you.

After a divorce there is a disruption in the relationship between parents and children; then, when a parent remarries, the children are forced to share this parent with another person and perhaps with other children as well. This is a change and a loss for the children. At the same time, they are gaining a stepparent, who may not be welcomed with open arms!

At the time of the remarriage, there also may be a move to a new community so that the children do not see their former friends and neighbors anymore. In addition, their place in the family may be totally changed as Johnnie suddenly becomes one of four children rather than an only child, or Suzy now a middle child rather than the cute youngest child.

Adjusting to all these changes is really hard for children, and they cannot enjoy the trips to the zoo, the picnics at the beach, or having more children to play with until they have had a chance to feel hurt and sad and angry about the losses and changes dropped into their lives.

For all members of a stepfamily it is helpful to talk about this sadness and not keep your sad feelings all bottled up because you think it might hurt the other members of your family. Perhaps some feelings need to be shared with your family. Perhaps some feelings need to be shared with your minister or rabbi, or doctor. However, it can be a relief for all family members to know that the sadness and upset felt because of all the changes and losses are understood and shared to some extent by other family members.

There are many expectations from former family experiences

Another characteristic that distinguishes stepfamilies from biological families is that each family member comes trailing behind him or her expectations and ways of doing things based on a number of previous family patterns.

Breakfast, lunch, and dinner—food—it sounds simple enough. But think for a moment of the variety of foods and how they are cooked! Do you eat meat? Is sugar a no-no? Are snacks allowed in the afternoon?

Betsy grew up until age ten in a family where her mother did the shopping and cooking. They ate meat, potatoes, and vegetables, followed by a yummy dessert if you had cleaned your plate. When Betsy was ten, her parents divorced, and the quality of the food in each single-parent household dropped drastically; in fact, in her father's house, Betsy considered his choice of TV dinners to be the absolute bottom.

After a couple of years, Betsy's father married a woman who was a gourmet cook and spent hours every day preparing cuisine that was a delight to Betsy's father, but made Betsy cranky and irritable. She had visions of Kentucky Fried Chicken and MacDonald's Big Macs floating before her eyes.

To compound the situation, Betsy's mother remarried a man who felt very concerned about the nutritional value of food and would not allow junk foods in the house. Whole grain replaced white flour, fish was substituted for meat, brown rice instead of mashed potatoes appeared on the dinner plates, and Betsy continued to dream of Big Macs and her mother's cinnamon rolls from the years before the divorce.

The choices in families are unlimited—whether to treasure or abhor animals, how to spend leisure weekend time, whether to turn the lights on and off and when, or how to put the roll of toilet paper in the holder!

When Phoebe married Charles, a first marriage for both, she complained, "I grew up in a family where my father was handy with tools and he fixed whatever went wrong around the house. Charles grew up in a family where he wasn't allowed to do anything like that. His family had lots of money and no one lifted a finger around the place. We get into terrible fights over spending money to pay someone to come in to fix our plugged drains and leaky toilet. I think Charles ought to learn how to do it and he won't. I'd rather have the money to go out to dinner or a show or something."

Phoebe and Charles found it necessary to negotiate expectations both had as a result of their experiences growing up with two different family patterns. In this first marriage, their two earlier families influenced Phoebe and Charles's expectations.

Phoebe and Charles had two children, and slowly they worked out ways of disciplining Mary and Amy, dividing work around the home, doing the laundry, cooking the meals, and so on. A family atmosphere slowly emerged.

Unfortunately, Phoebe and Charles began to experience many difficulties in getting along together and after seven years they were divorced. Mary and Amy continued to live primarily with their mother and spent alternate weekends and certain holiday periods with their father.

At the end of three years Phoebe married a widower, Rick, who had one son, Rolly. These two adults and the three children—five different people—came together with varying expectations of when to go to bed, where to put the television, how to light a fire, bake cookies, make pancakes, drive a car, and celebrate holidays.

These expectations came from many different family experiences:

1. The family Phoebe grew up in.
2. Phoebe's first marriage family.
3. The single-parent household containing Phoebe and her two children.

4. The family Rick grew up in.
5. Rick's first marriage family.
6. The single-parent household containing Rick and his son Rolly.

And now with this new marriage the new stepfamily has to work out its own traditions and ways of doing things, and everyone wants and needs a say in where the dog sleeps, who feeds the cat, how to share the telephone, what happens on Thanksgiving Day. There are six previous family patterns bumping along together or clashing head on as this new family unit works out its own standard operating procedures. It's easy to see why it takes time and energy.

There are parent-child relationships that were there before the couple got together

Phyllis and Jason met in the skies over Chicago. They both worked for the same airline, and their romance soared higher than the planes on which they flew! They were married within five months and then a reality which they had not expected suddenly brought them down to earth. Phyllis had been married before and had two children who spent half of each month with her. Not until after they were married did Jason meet his wife's children, his new stepchildren. Beth, aged eight, and Charlie, nine, were charming children who wondered why this strange man was living in their house all the time, and they felt the need to compete with him for time with their mother. Meanwhile, Jason felt totally isolated and Phyllis felt guilty about asking her children to accept her new relationship with Jason. She tried very hard to keep the household on an even keel, but she shared many years of common memories with her children while Jason was the newcomer and outsider. Jason and Phyllis also had shared experiences not shared by the children, but their five months together seemed tentative and transient when compared with the almost nine years Phyllis and her children had shared.

It took this stepfamily a number of months to overcome these differences, get acquainted with each other, and begin to do things together to create their own shared memories and personal relationships. If they had started out by introducing all future stepfamily members to each other and doing things together *before* the marriage took place, they could have helped blur these time-related alliances.

Unlike a first marriage in which the couple has a relationship before adding a child to the family, in stepfamilies there are relationships between parents and children that existed before the new couple got together. Perhaps you and your wife have been married for three years, and she and her children were together for four years between her divorce and your remarriage. Her daughter, Lisa, is 12, and her son, Gordon, is 10. Your couple relationship is the new one and may be very delicate compared to the older parent-child alliances. When your stepson blinks his eyes three times, his mother may know just what he means, but you wonder what's going on. When Lisa shrugs her shoulders, her mother knows she's saying, "I don't care, either way is fine," but to you it seems like she's saying, "Nuts to you, who do you think you are?" It's a long-standing communication system with which you're not familiar.

There seems no time for you and your wife to be together. No romantic moments in front of the fire. No leisurely Sunday mornings in bed. Lisa and Gordon are always there, butting in, asking questions, needing help. And your wife doesn't seem to mind. She's grown up with these two, and you are on the outside, an intruding act trying to break into a three-ring circus.

Lisa and Gordon feel left out when you two adults do things without them, and your wife gets angry at you, at them, and at the crumbs on the kitchen floor. She may be feeling caught in the middle, wanting to build a close relationship with you but feeling guilty that she is neglecting her children if she does this. Changing the relationship patterns in the household is very important and often takes conscious thought and effort to accomplish. Here are a few suggestions that have worked for a number of stepfamilies:

- Build up your newer couple relationship by planning outings alone such as going out to dinner, taking a drive, riding bicycles, walking on the beach, arranging special nights or weekends without the children.
- Provide the children with a feeling that there is still a special relationship with their own parent so that they will then more easily

accept new relationship patterns. This can be done by having parent and child, or parent and children, continue previous activities they enjoyed together—for example, shopping, working in the garden, reading stories, or playing checkers.

- Build new adult-child relationships by having stepparent and stepchild do together activities that are fun—going out to get ice cream cones or hamburgers, playing games, working on model airplanes, making doll clothes, cooking together.
- Build up relationships between stepbrothers and stepsisters by arranging for them to do things together which they enjoy.
- Plan together activities for the entire family unit, but don't expect full participation from teenagers, since adolescents in *all* types of families often don't wish to be part of such "family" outings.

Flexibility also helps in building new relationship patterns. Take advantage of the opportunities that arise spontaneously. When a parent goes to the grocery store, the stepparent left at home may invite his or her stepchild to play a game or help wash the car. Or, stepmother and stepson may find themselves enjoying a television program while the rest of the family is busy elsewhere. Or, when the children are with friends for the afternoon, the couple can enjoy the intimacy they need to nourish their own relationship. However, don't depend on circumstances—you will probably need to schedule time to build new relationships.

There is a former spouse, the other biological parent, who has an influence on the stepfamily

While all families are influenced by persons and events outside their specific family unit, the fact that there is a former spouse, another biological parent, outside the particular stepfamily unit creates ambiguity and feelings of helplessness and lack of control that first marriages usually do not have. You may wonder if Johnnie's father will return him on time so that you, your new husband, Johnnie and his half-sister Jill can catch the plane for your trip to Bermuda. Or will Mary's mother remember to send a party dress with Mary this weekend so she will have something appropriate to wear to the birthday party she has been invited to while she's staying with you and her father?

As one stepmother said, "I never know what I can count on. We got all ready to go to the beach and the kids show up four hours later." Another remarried mother says, "My ex likes to have the children all dressed up with their hair brushed and combed. So I get them all dressed up and make them stay in the house for hours, and their father sails in three hours late. It doesn't make sense to the kids that they have to stay in the house for ages dressed up to the teeth so they won't dirty." A remarried father, feeling helpless and angry, complains bitterly, "No matter how much money I dish out, it never seems enough to Annie's mother, and Annie comes crying to me that she has to have a little hamburger and can't have a Big Mac when she goes to MacDonald's because I don't send her mommy enough money."

Lucy never told her children, who were 11 and 12, when their father, Tony, was coming to take them for an outing, because Tony would promise to be there at five and show up at 6:30—or he would phone and say he couldn't make it after all. Lucy knew it was important not to say angry things to the children about her ex-husband, since he was their father and they loved him. So more and more she began to protect her children from knowing what Tony had said he would do for them, and more and more Lucy grew angry and bitter—feelings which came out in little ways. The children were bewildered, wondering what was making their mother so cranky, and wishing they knew enough to make plans for the weekends.

Finally Lucy's anger boiled over and she let her children know how bothered she was that Tony didn't make plans ahead and didn't pick them up when he said he would. Now the children understood their mother's frustration and annoyance, and much to her surprise they laughed, "Oh, that's just the way Dad is!" Then Lucy relaxed, kept herself out of the middle, and let the children know what was supposed to happen. The kids related directly with their father on the telephone and worked out together what sort of relationship they would have with him.

This other adult may have a lot of influence on what happens with your children and the plans you make. If the adults can work plans together over the phone, by letter, or however feels most comfortable, then your children will not be so caught in the middle and usually will not complain so much. If you find that the adults in both households are not able to do this, a counselor or social worker may be able to help you work out a communication system that does not involve the children as messengers or adversely affect their relationships with parents or stepparents.

Another way to bring these difficult family situations under control is to think about what you yourselves can do without ever having to involve the biological parent in the other household. For example, instead of keeping the children all dressed up and waiting, you can have their clean clothes ready and when their father does arrive he can wait a few minutes while the children come in from playing and get changed. Or you can make it clear to the children and their other parent that you are leaving to go to the beach at a specified time and if the children are not there yet you will leave a note on the door letting them know when you will be back, where you are in case your former husband wants to drop them off at the beach, or what neighbor is home and willing to have the children play until your return.

Obviously, there are many different situations and many different ways of figuring out what may work out best. People often make the mistake of thinking that there are "perfect" solutions to problems. This is generally not true and so they get upset and feel disappointed. Others repeatedly blame the former spouse and demand that he or she change. However, if both adults or, whenever possible, adults and children in your stepfamily attempt to work out the best solutions, then you will find there are many situations you can work out for yourselves and you won't feel so helpless, so lacking in control, and so angry.

Even when the former spouse has died, the impact of that person can still be felt in the household. If you have married a widow or widower, you may find that your partner is still trying to do everything "the way Lenore wanted it done," or that "Charlie liked to have Sunday supper this way." And it may seem to the children involved that you, if you are a remarried parent, didn't really love their father or mother, or if you are a stepparent, that you are trying to take their dead parent's place and make them forget that other parent.

Often, too, as time goes by, the person who has died is remembered for all the wonderful things that he or she did. People talk about all the times the dead spouse worked hard, was unselfish and loving. Forgotten are the times when that he or she was tired and cranky, drank too much, or didn't measure up in some way. In this way the former spouse becomes a "saint" and you, the stepparent, may begin to feel more and more inadequate, as you are compared unfavorably to the idealized person who is no longer alive and acting in a human way—happy one day, cross and discouraged another day. It's hard to remember that this other person was a human being too, and that if you can keep calm, the shining memories you are hearing may get tucked into a corner where they will gather enough dust to lose their unnatural luster. Feeling free to talk about the person who has died can relieve a tension that would otherwise build up if there is a prohibition, either spoken or felt, against mentioning the former spouse and parent.

The children belong to two different households

In original families everyone is pretty clear about where the family boundary is. While your children are "living at home" and still going to school, everyone in the particular household who is blood related or legally related is considered "family." Perhaps Aunt Clara is living with you too—then she is considered part of the family. Even when your children move out and are working and/or married, or continuing their education in another geographic area, they are still considered part of your family. Bob may be in Africa in the Peace Corps, but yours is still his home and his family. Of course, many relatives can be considered part of the "family" if you consider extended families and kinship groups.

For stepfamilies, in contrast, family boundaries are hazy and confused. A few stepfamilies consider in-laws, ex-in-laws, spouses, ex-spouses, and various assortments of step-relatives and former relatives as one form of an "extended" family. The usual situation, however, is for two separate family units to overlap through the children, thus conferring on the children the dubious honor of belonging to two different households. This dual membership really *can* be an honor because it can give children more adult role models to choose from and pattern themselves after, and it provides children with a richness of experiences which could not be provided by only one household. Unfortunately, all too often children feel pulled apart and torn by loyalty conflicts because of the existence of two households; yet, if there is no separation between the children's two households, the confusion and conflicting feelings of the adults involved add to rather than lessen the insecurities of children.

Studies show that, whenever possible, children need to maintain a relationship with both of their biological parents. Sometimes they do not see one parent very often, but even a little contact lets the children know that they are not unloved by the less available parent. There is still a relationship and this is very important to children.

You can visualize the situation in the following way:

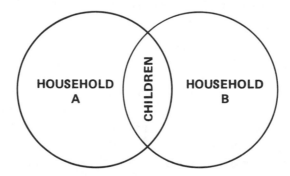

Let's say that yours is Household A. No doubt you have rules in your household that are different from the regulations and expectations in Household B. No two households can be exactly the same since the people in them have all come from different backgrounds and have different ways of doing things. Your children need to shift their behavior when they go from your household to Household B, and then they need to shift again when they return to your household. Some children experience what they often call "culture shock" as they go back and forth from one household to the other. These changes make them uncomfortable and often cranky. If you let your children have a little time to settle in to your routine without expecting them to switch easily and quickly, things will go much more smoothly! And if it's okay for them to say they have had a good time in Household B, they can relax more easily and enjoy your household too.

If it is not clear to your children that there are two separate households, and that they are the only individuals who belong in both households, then their fantasies of bringing their two biological parents together again often remain active. The adults in your two households must cooperate over visiting arrangements, vacation plans, or holiday celebrations; at the same time it can be clear that each household has its own boundaries. For example, you may arrange with the adult or adults in Household B to have all the children with you for a certain weekend. What you do on that weekend is for your household to decide, plan, and enjoy, while the plans carried out by the individuals in Household B for the same weekend are made in that household without consultation with you.

Perhaps insecurity and jealousy are the two most difficult reactions parents and stepparents have to deal with because there are these two households. You may find yourself wondering if your children care more about being with their other parent, or their other parent and stepparent, than they do about being with you and your new spouse or partner. Do they have more fun when they are away from you? Will they know you love them even though you can't take them to Disneyland or buy them the expensive toys they receive in their other household? Is their stepparent a better cook than you are? Does their stepparent read stories better than you do? Does it seem to the children that the parent who sees them only on weekends has time to play, while you are always rushing off to work?

It is very, very hard not to have such questions and equally difficult to keep from feeling insecure and discouraged. As a result, you may tell your children not to talk to you about what they do when they are away from you, or, on the other hand, you may ask them questions about what they did on the weekend, all the time hoping that they will say everything was terrible. Sharing children stirs up many deep feelings of insecurity which are picked up by the children so that they are uncomfortable swinging back and forth between the two households. We have found that if you are able to give your children permission to care about all the parental adults in their lives and to enjoy both their households, they have fewer loyalty pulls; as a result, they enjoy their

Because children are part of two biological parents they nearly always have very strong pulls to both parents. These divided loyalties often make it difficult for children to relate comfortably to all the parental adults in their lives. Rejection of a stepparent, for example, may have nothing to do with the personal characteristics of the stepparent. In fact, warm and loving stepparents may cause especially severe loyalty conflicts for children. As children and adults are able to accept the fact that children can care for more than two parental adults, then the children's loyalty conflicts can diminish and the new step-relationships improve. While it may be helpful to the children for the adults to acknowledge negative as well as positive feelings about ex-spouses, children may become caught in loyalty conflicts and feel personally insecure if specific critical remarks are made continuously about their other parent.

relationships with you more than ever—because they can let you know what they are doing, and they can speak spontaneously without having to filter out things they feel will make you unhappy. In turn, you can feel more relaxed because your children are less tense, more cheerful and cooperative, and not "driving you up the wall."

Bill and Clara have been married for three years. Clara has not been married before, but Bill has two children, Billy, five, and Barbara, eight, who spend a major part of the time with their mother Joyce, Bill's ex-wife, and her husband Paul. However, Billy and Barbara also spend some weekends and vacation times with Bill and Clara. Bill, Clara, Joyce and Paul talk together from time to time to coordinate plans, and Billy and Barbara enjoy both households very much. Each adult has very special talents and warmth to give to the children: Bill is a whiz at helping with the children's interest in space toys; Clara enjoys working with puppets; Joyce is a librarian and puts her knowledge of children's books to good use; and Paul loves the out-of-doors and makes very interesting plans for overnights or walks on the beach to gather shells.

Billy and Barbara spend time in each household, helping with the necessary daily chores, doing their homework, watching TV, and also taking advantage of the variety of talents and activities offered to them by the different adults in their lives. There is plenty of caring to go around! And the adults do not feel a need to compete with one another or to try to take away the pleasure which the children have in each relationship.

Stepparents and stepchildren are not legally related to each other

Biological parents have legal rights in relationship to their children that stepparents do not have. For many stepfamilies this difference makes for minor annoyances only—for example, a stepparent cannot legally sign a permission slip for an overnight camping trip for a stepchild or sign for a driver's permit for a 16-year-old stepchild.

More serious is the situation that can arise if you have a minor stepchild who has an accident and needs medical attention requiring parental permission. Unless you have a prior agreement with your local hospital, your signature as a stepparent is very often not acceptable. Naturally, in life-threatening situations a physician will give the needed attention regardless of who is with the child, but many stepparents have complained about their lack of authority in lesser emergencies.

Some hospitals have their own forms that can be signed by the parents or parent with custody, granting permission for stepparents and/or other caretaking adults to sign for minor children. Authorization may be granted by having your attorney write a simple statement such as the one given on the next page.

Sometimes parents feel that signing such a form giving a stepparent this authority threatens their own control regarding their children. If this is true in your situation, it will often reduce the tense feelings if you also include other caretaking people such as grandparents, your family doctor and/or the child's school principal as authorized persons. Do-

MEDICAL AND DENTAL AUTHORIZATION
(California Civil Code Section 25.8)

The undersigned, _____ *Mary Jones* _____
who resides at _____ *10 Applewood Way, Saratoga, California* _____,
and the undersigned, _____ *John Brown* _____, who
resides at _____ *46 Newport Road, San Jose, California* _____, and
who are the parents who have legal custody of _____ *Timothy Brown* _____,
a minor, and _____ *Janet Brown* _____, a minor, herein authorize
_____ *Charlotte Brown* _____, an adult person into whose care
_____ *Timothy Brown* _____ and _____ *Janet Brown* _____
have been entrusted and who resides at _____ *46 Newport Road,* _____
_____ *San Jose, California* _____ to consent to any x-ray examination, anesthetic, medical or surgical diagnosis or treatment and hospital care, to be rendered to either of said minors under the general or special supervision and upon the advice of a physician and surgeon licensed under the provisions of the California Medicine Practice Act, and to consent to an x-ray examination, anesthetic, dental or surgical diagnosis or treatment and hospital care, to be rendered to either of said minors by a dentist licensed under the provisions of the California Dental Practice Act.

Dated: _____

Witness:

_____   _____

_____   _____

ing this indicates more clearly that the stepparent is not trying to reduce the biological parent's control, but is seeking to insure the welfare of the children in an emergency.

There are two major difficulties that can arise from this lack of legal relationship. The first is the fear that the stepparent may feel in forming too close a relationship with a stepchild. If you have experienced previous losses of personal or family relationships, your fear of losing the new step-relationships may be particularly strong, since the step-relationship lasts only as long as the marriage lasts. This fear, then, may make you hold back from responding warmly to your stepchild or stepchildren, and this pulling back can negatively affect the way your stepfamily functions. You pull back, your stepchild pulls back, your partner feels torn and angry, and a negative downward spiral is underway.

It is important to take the risk and work to build a strong stepparent-stepchild relationship. We have found that even after a second divorce many former stepparents and stepchildren continue their relationships without legal ties of any kind. A piece of paper cannot create a relationship or destroy it. In addition, the legal profession is beginning to recognize that the laws are not keeping up with the changes in family patterns, and attention is being given to this ambiguous area.

The other serious difficulty that can arise from the lack of a legal stepparent-stepchild relationship occurs when the child's biological parent dies. For example, a mother and her two children, Lila and Laura, and their stepfather have been a family unit for over 10 years. Lila and Laura are now 14 and 12 and during one month each summer they visit with their biological father and his new wife. Suddenly their mother dies. Unless the girls' biological father agrees, legally Lila and Laura cannot stay in the home in which they have grown up, with the man with whom they have had a long and close relationship, even if that is his desire and the wish of the girls. In situations such as this, laws are slowly changing in many states to ease the heartache that can be caused by the present legal restrictions.

Because of these complications you may be thinking of adopting your stepchildren. In some instances such a course of action may work out well, but our experience with adoptions indicates that adoption of stepchildren is an extremely complicated emotional issue and needs to be given very careful consideration. Indeed, this is an area where exploration with a counselor can be of great benefit because of the deep feelings involved—for you, for the child, and for others in your family. Adoption can settle some legal questions, but, contrary to many people's expectations, adoption of a stepchild does not necessarily settle uncomfortable relationships within the family unit.

When they become independent adults, many adopted stepchildren seek out their biological parents with whom they may have lost contact; in some instances they legally change their name back to their original birth name if there had been a change at the time of the adoption. Biological "roots" are powerful, and we need to know much more about the short-term and long-term effects of stepchild adoption to provide guidelines in this area. Fortunately, there is a growing interest in systematically studying adoption issues. This means that more information will become available for those stepparents and remarried parents considering this possibility. We do know that adoption is not necessary for close emotional ties to develop between stepparents and stepchildren.

Why it is important to realize that there are different types of families

There are a variety of family models, each with its own characteristics, its own joys and sorrows, its own challenges and rewards. The differences between family types necessarily produce different situations and different feelings.

If you forget that there are differences between your stepfamily and a first marriage family, you may keep trying to fit your present family into the family "model" you have had in your imagination for many, many years. This can cause a lot of pressure for you and for everyone in the family, and a tremendous sense of failure for all of you. The Ugly Duckling was in despair until he looked at himself in the mirror of a lake and discovered and accepted that he was, in fact, a swan and not a duck at all. Nowhere does it say that only one type of family can look in the mirror and see healthy, happy children and fulfilled adults. Stepfamilies are what they are. They have their own set of characteristics and, as in any type of family, the family members can learn what to expect and therefore learn how to make their particular type of family work for them.

2 | Loss — Single-Parent Households — Dating

Because the formation of a stepfamily follows the loss or disruption of a couple relationship and a time of living in a single-parent household, what happens during these preceding periods can greatly influence how the new stepfamily functions. Adults often rush into new long-term relationships or marriages with poor preparation during the time they have been with their children in a single-parent household or before they have allowed themselves time to say their good-byes to the past.

Even if you are already remarried, you may find it helpful to consider if there are ways in which events during the months or years when you were a single parent may be affecting you and your present family. If there are blocks in your path coming from these times, recognizing them can help you make some changes in dealing with your present situation so as to bring more satisfaction to you and your family.

The first months after the death
of a spouse

For some months after the death of a spouse, the remaining partner has to deal with many deep and powerful emotions, including anger, guilt, depression, and extreme loneliness. Friends and relatives may have been wonderful and helped you a great deal, but eventually they have given all the support they know how to give or can give. The time comes when they go back to taking care of their own lives and their own families.

Your children may be reacting strongly to the death of their parent, and they need support and comfort at the same time that you do.It is helpful if you can all cry together and share your anger, and guilt, and unhappiness. Even if you are able to do this, you and your children may want to talk with a counselor who is specially trained to help families at such times. If you and your children are not able to share your feelings with one another, then it is most important to have an outside person or persons for support—a minister, a rabbi, a counselor, a widow or widower's group—to lean on for awhile, and also to give to in terms of sharing your own experiences.

It is a temptation for parents to lean on their children after the death of a partner, particularly if the children are in their teens. It can happen when the children are much younger, too, and it cuts the children off from the support they need from you. Grandparents are often very comforting for adults and children alike, but you may need additional adult support if your parents or in-laws are unavailable to you and your children. Even if you or your children have had a poor or very confused relationship with the person who has died, the hope of a changed and improved relationship is now lost, and so you may be experiencing as strong a mixture of emotions as you would if the relationship had been a very positive one.

There is a "widow-to-widow" program, and there are groups in many areas brought together through Adult Education Services, religious institutions, YWCA, YMCA, or Family Services Agencies. There are also books written to give you needed understanding and support, so that you and your children can cope with your loss and begin to reach out once again for new relationships.

The first months after a divorce

Unfortunately, the support given by your community and by your friends after a death usually is missing if you have just gone through the trauma of a divorce and the loss of a relationship which was very important to you at some time in the past. Even if you wanted the divorce and have a sense of relief, there may be many feelings of sadness and loss for you. In addition, your children may be very upset. One young child had experienced the death of her father and was now experiencing the divorce of her mother and stepfather. The day after her stepfather left, the little girl, remembering the house full of friends and neighbors after her father's death, turned to her mother and said through her tears, "Where are all the people?"

There are a number of things you can do to make these months easier for yourself and for your children. If you have moved out of your home, don't settle for a dreary little spot on a dirty sidestreet. Surround yourself with an atmosphere that is cheerful and pleasant. You need to give yourself this type of space so that you can go through the numbness, then the pain and hurt, anger, guilt, sadness and eventual healing helped by an environment that will support, not hinder, the process.

You also need to take care of yourself, for the sake of your children. They need to know that you have upset feelings just as they do, but they also need to have you continue to be an important person in their eyes. Children are affected by where you live, as is illustrated by a conversation grown children had together as they talked about their earlier years:

Barbie B: "For me it was the divorce that was hard. I remember that first Christmas after the divorce. We spent time with Daddy in

Phoenix. I remember it because of his tiny little apartment. It was so dismal over there."

Les L. : "I felt bad about my Dad's apartment just as you did about your father's apartment. Dad moved out and moved into a small, miserable place. It had a glass door between the bedroom and kitchen, and the ceilings felt like they were crushing down they were so low. It seemed dark, and then somehow it got connected in my mind with Dad's being defeated, being dethroned."

Even if you must scrimp financially, try to live in a cheerful spot with plants and pictures, music and color—whatever gives you pleasure.

If you remain in your home, you may be faced suddenly with many bare spots or empty rooms as a spouse and, perhaps, the children move out. Fill in those gaps creatively so that the loss is less acute and the process of healing can begin more rapidly. An empty room that is a constant reminder of loss can become a space full of life as you change it into a hobby spot or into a playroom with all those formerly scattered toys and games that can now have a spot of their own.

Activity helps your body and lightens your mood. Exercise in ways you find comfortable.

Discard possessions that produce pain for you. If they are family heirlooms, you may wish to put them away for a later time. If they represent monetary value only, disposing of them may cost you much less pain than keeping them around.

Social contacts can restore self-esteem and give you a rest from the strong emotions you may be feeling. People often make the mistake of thinking that you can get rid of bad feelings by telling yourself not to think about them. Every time you say to yourself, "I am going to stop feeling sad," you think about feeling sad again! To stop feeling sad, you need to put some other thoughts and feelings inside your head. Replace thoughts that are tearing you down with other, more pleasant thoughts growing out of pleasurable activities. You can concentrate on only one thing at a time. So if you like sports, watch a ballgame or a tennis match. If you like nature, go for a walk and really notice the sky and the trees or whatever is around you. If you enjoy people, plan an activity—even the anticipation of the event can drive away your dwelling on unwanted repetitive thoughts and emotions.

You need support at this time, and there are many services available for divorced adults—discussion groups, therapy groups, singles groups of all kinds (religious, supportive, activity oriented, social). There are fewer groups for children, but many school counselors and family doctors can offer helpful suggestions at such a time.

There are also books to help you and your children understand what is happening. These offer reassurance, which helps in dealing with the loss and then moving on to new relationships and new experiences. See Appendix B for helpful books, or write to the Stepfamily Association of America, Inc., 215 Centennial Mall S., Suite 212, Lincoln, NE, 68508. Also, try your local library.

Single-parent households

Various studies have shown that after a divorce children grow and mature in a more satisfactory manner if they are able to maintain some contact with *both* of their biological parents.

If your relationship with your ex-spouse is angry and hostile, it is difficult not to fight over visitation and custody issues. Your children will be happier, will grow into adulthood much more easily, and will be much more fun for you to be with if you keep any battles with your ex-spouse between the adults only. Children of all ages become very upset when they are put in the middle between their two parents, carrying messages back and forth, being asked to choose where they want to be (unless they are adolescents), or being "pumped" by you or your ex-spouse for information about what is taking place in the other household. Do your best to deal directly with your ex-spouse in person, on the telephone, or by letter (whichever works out best for you and your children). In this way, your children can be more relaxed and living with them will be a lot easier!

If you have been able to work out satisfactory arrangements with your ex-spouse regarding your children's continued contact with both of you, you will have provided some stability for your children during these times of many family changes.

One divorced mother stated it this way: "Sending Timmy off to kindergarten was hard because it was the beginning of separating myself from him. I realize now that sharing him with his father now that we are divorced is more of the same separation process. It will continue as Timmy graduates from high school and goes out on his own. But it's hard for me now because it's so much sooner and I didn't expect it to happen this way. I haven't had time to get prepared for it slowly."

It is difficult to "share" children, but it often becomes easier as you get more used to your new living arrangements. If you are still working out living arrangements for your children with your former partner, it is worthwhile to take the time to try new and possibly more satisfactory arrangements. The fact that you and your ex-spouse are not able to live together does not mean that you cannot respect each other's parenting ability. Even if your parenting styles are very different, children can benefit from many different ways of doing things, and can get different needs met by one or the other of their two parents. Children don't necessarily need to have the same needs met by each parent.

It has been said that single-parent households are emotionally overloaded households if there are children living there a major part of the time. One parent is now carrying the full load of adult responsibility for the household, and the burden can be very heavy unless you have sufficient money to pay others to help you with the daily requirements of running a household—shopping, cooking, cleaning, doing the laundry, chauffeuring the children, fixing everything that breaks, mowing the lawn, reading bedtime stories to young children, packing lunches —to mention only a few of the tasks!

Unfortunately, money is usually a problem in a single-parent household, and it is easy to see why the household burdens can become overwhelming. For most single-parent households the adult is also holding down a fulltime job outside of the household, on top of everything else!

While you will need to tackle the household tasks, perhaps learning new tasks that were done by your former spouse, you will no doubt get more cooperation from your children if you all work together to figure out who is going to do what. Be easy on yourself and your children. Some things you have to do to keep yourself and your children healthy —putting foods in the refrigerator which might spoil; brushing your teeth to avoid getting cavities. However, many tasks are not essential to future life and happiness. Ask yourself which ones on the list you prepare are really important! Blondie the dog *does* need to have water and food, but couldn't care less if she is bathed every other week instead of weekly. In fact, she might enjoy a respite from bathing while you use the time for something more important.

Parents Without Partners is a national organization which often is of great help to individuals in single-parent households. Social events provide support and also help with the loneliness and isolation that is so often felt by one adult alone in a household.

Babysitting cooperatives are springing up to fill the crucial need for child care where funds do not allow one to have this most necessary service. If there is no cooperative in your neighborhood, you may want to find other single parents who would like to "trade hours" and help you establish your own informal child care cooperative. If you decide to do this, be sure you all have the rules spelled out in writing so that no upset feelings occur because some individuals find it easier to use the "service" than to repay their debt of time to the group, or fail to provide the kind of child care which is adequate. For example, you may want to allow only a certain number of hours of receiving "service" to accumulate before the hours are repaid.

There are a number of books that deal with this period of parenting with day-to-day help from the other parent. Even if you or your ex-spouse have already remarried you may find helpful material for yourself in this book: *Mom's House, Dad's House* by Isolina Ricci.

Leaving room for other people to join your household

At first, after death of a spouse or a divorce, there is a wide gap in the family circle. Slowly this spot is filled in with changed relationships between parent and children, new activities and greater time spent on former activities. Often parents turn to their children for the emotional support that is now missing as a result of the loss of a partner. You need to continue friendships and activities you previously enjoyed and perhaps explore other areas you feel you might enjoy. Forming a close bond with your children is certainly beneficial for all of you. However, it is easy to begin to lean on your children as "substitute" partners and to form such a tight unit that it is very difficult for any of you to let another person into your lives. There is just not room for another person to squeeze into this closed circle of you and your children.

Ellen married Bill who had two children from a previous marriage. Depressed after his divorce, Bill had spent weekends and all his vacation time relating to his two children. The three of them played games, camped together over long weekends, and were constantly on the go. Bill dated only when his children were not with him.

When Bill and Ellen were married, the children and Bill continued their activity patterns together, and were reluctant to have Ellen join them. They seemed to feel that she just didn't fit in. Ellen had not been previously interested in sports or camping, but she was willing to try since she wanted to become a part of the group. The children, however, didn't want to change and Bill felt guilty when he suggested that Ellen be included or that they plan something else where she would be on more familiar ground. Thus, there was little space for Ellen to become part of the family outings.

In contrast, when Agnes and Eric were married, Agnes had little difficulty being absorbed into Eric's family. After his divorce Eric had dealt with his loneliness by participating in a wide variety of activities. When his two children were with him, they often took friends along on family camping trips, and sometimes their friends came to stay on weekends when Eric had other plans. After their marriage, Eric and Agnes continued to include the children's friends from time to time, and since the group had always been variable and flexible, Agnes soon found a place for herself in the new family unit.

This may not be of concern to you because you have no intention of remarrying. Many widowed and divorced people do remarry. Therefore, you may find yourself changing your mind later on, and leaving spaces for new people will then have been helpful. Even if you do not remarry, your children need independent growing space so that they can go on to fulfilling adult lives and relationships.

If there is little space in your relationship with your children, the following may happen:

- You will not date.
- You will not form a new partner relationship.

- Your children will become very upset if you start dating because they will feel replaced.
- If you remarry, there will be no space for the new person and he or she will not become a part of the family. This can often lead to another separation and divorce.

There are many ways in which to avoid forming such an impenetrable unit. If you believe that you have already slipped into such a closed parent-child group, whether or not you are remarried, you can use the following suggestions to help to alter the situation. These will help you make steady but gradual shifts in the direction of loosening the circle so that there is space for other people in your lives.

- Have friends of your children at your house to play with them.
- Encourage your children to do things with their friends.
- Entertain friends at your home rather than always being there alone with your family.
- Include others in some of your recreational activities. For example, go with your children and friends of theirs, or of yours, or both, on a picnic, or to the movies, or to have pizza.
- Do not expect any of your children to take over as "the man of the house" or the "woman of the house" or make comments to them about doing this.
- Do things with your new partner or with your friends that do not include your children. If your children are young, get a baby-sitter or trade with another family if you cannot afford a sitter.
- Encourage your children to participate in activities they show an interest in—but do not push them so that they feel they are doing it for *you* rather than for themselves.
- Take time for yourself, even when you are at home and your children are there. Relax in ways you enjoy—either alone or with your new spouse if you are remarried.

Keep in mind that all of the above suggestions apply no matter how much time your children are in your household with you—a weekend, a month, or three weeks of every month. In other words, find constructive and enjoyable ways in which to lead a life of your own and have your children enjoy the parts of their lives that are separate from yours. Sometimes include others in the things you all do together, and if you have a new adult relationship take the necessary time away from the children to nourish that relationship.

Dating

It is a very individual matter when a widowed or divorced person feels like dating. Taking time to relinquish your strong emotional ties to the past needs to precede serious involvements or the past intrudes on the present and your new relationships seldom work out well. This is not to say that memories of the past die or are forgotten—a scent, a certain song, or a familiar place may always stir deep or nostalgic memories. However, for the most part, when you are ready to date seriously your attention and focus are on the present and future. If you have children, they act as a link to your former marriage, but even when you are in contact with their other parent, there does not need to be continued personal involvement that interferes with new interpersonal relationships.

When a parent has died, older children often have difficulty when their remaining parent begins to date. To the children it may seem that you did not really care about their dead parent. It is reassuring to children to say to them clearly that such is not the case (if indeed you did care about your former spouse), and that no other relationship will be the same as that earlier relationship, because no other person is the same as their other parent was. You may need to repeat this message many times, and even though your children may attempt to stop you from dating other people by saying they do not believe you, it is not in their best interest or in your best interest to close yourself off from adult companionship. Your children may remain angry for a while, but that is better than having them feel guilty and worried about growing up and leading their own lives away from a sad and lonely parent.

After a divorce, a great many children hang on to the fantasy that their parents will get back together again. In fact, children often act in totally obnoxious ways when their parent has a date in the hopes that this unwelcome intruder will quickly retreat. Other children promote dating because they've decided they want a new parent, and then change their minds after the marriage has taken place and their dreams of constant attention and care are shattered.

Gradual changes are easier for people of all ages to handle. It usually works better if, when you start dating, you are not away from your children for long periods of time. At the same time, you should not try to hide the fact that you are dating from them or plan all your dates for times when they will be visiting their other parent. If they are used to having you away for an evening, or a day and evening, they will not feel devastated and abandoned when you decide to take a week's vacation without them. Of course, if they can stay with their other parent, with relatives, or with a familiar and loved baby-sitter, the time you spend away from them may often be more pleasant for everyone for this brief period of separation.

It is generally better to have an easy, ongoing relationship with another adult before you include your children in your activities with that person. Introducing everyone at once and doing things together before anyone feels comfortable does not encourage relationship-building. Little Charlie crawling under the table while Suzie is screaming that she wants a hamburger is hardly conducive to cementing a new relationship!

People are often surprised at the strong reaction which an ex-spouse may have when he or she learns, usually from the children, that the other parent is beginning to date or is developing a new serious relationship. Do not be surprised if this happens and your children start telling you about this new person in their lives. You may be afraid that he or she will try to "lure" them away, and it is difficult not to feel threatened by this new parental-type person unless you are very secure in your own parenting abilities. Also, if you are the one with the new adult relationship, you may find that your ex-spouse may exhibit signs of being upset and even a little jealous. Even though he or she may have been the one who wanted the divorce, he or she may feel deep down that you were not going to get involved with anyone else or were not capable of it.

It is important to explain very clearly to your children that your new relationship does not mean that you are replacing their other parent. They may have to hear several times that their other parent will always be their parent, and that a new spouse will never take the place of their parent. It is very important for children to maintain contact with their other parent as they grow older.

Your children may ask you over and over if you are going to marry Agnes, or Jim, or whoever your current date may be. It is not helpful for them to think that you are seriously involved with another person if you are unsure of your commitment to that person, because children experience a loss whenever they have grown to care about someone and then that person disappears, only to be replaced with someone new. If these losses happen for your children more than a few times, you may find them unwilling to be pleasant to a new person you are dating. The children do not wish to experience the pain of loss again, and so they may withdraw and even act in an obnoxious way towards the new person to guard against caring and then losing again. So try to be cautious in giving the message that a relationship may become a permanent one until the two of you feel a deep sense of commitment to one another.

Having a new adult stay overnight

Unlike a few decades ago when rules and standards of behavior were spelled out clearly and accepted by the majority of people in the United States, codes of conduct now shift rapidly and are anything but uniform throughout the country. The rising divorce rate and the changing roles for men and women in America have produced a variety of new dating and relationship patterns, as well as a sexual freedom unknown even in the recent past.

Changes also produce confusion, and at this time we know of no systematic studies which provide guidelines for decisions in this area of having a new person spend the night with you when your children are also staying or living with you. From working with a number of families and from talking with others who work with all types of families, there do seem to be a few helpful guidelines:

1. Be clear inside yourself what messages you want your children to receive about relationships between partners. If your children see a number of different partners staying overnight with you during a relatively short period of time, they will receive the message that such behavior is not necessarily related to a sustained relationship. If, on the other hand, someone whom you are close to emotionally and with

whom your children also feel comfortable stays overnight with you, this conveys the message that emotional commitment is involved.

2. It is difficult for young children to form close attachments to new adults who move into your home and then leave after a period of time. You cannot always know how a relationship will eventually turn out, but erring on the conservative side when it comes to having new partners move in—and then move out—can save sadness and heartache on the part of your children. They have already experienced losses of individuals to whom they have become attached, and too many experiences of loss can lead your children to withdraw from getting involved emotionally with others because of the pain they begin to associate with such involvement. There is a great deal of individual variation in the reactions of children to sexual observations and ideas—depending on age, past experience, geographic area of residence, and general levels of maturity. Each parent needs to consider these factors carefully in making a decision. Be careful not to let your own enthusiasm blind you to caution signals flashed to you by your children.

3. Unless they are very "sophisticated" for their age, children under the age of nine to ten are not apt to be aware of the sexual aspects of your relationships in the same emotional way as are older children who are aware of their own emerging sexuality. It is known that teenage girls have a particularly difficult time handling their mothers' sexuality after a divorce. In biological families, children tend to regard their parents as nonsexual beings, while in single-parent households, as well as in stepfamilies, adolescents are no longer able to escape the sexual implications of their parents' new relationships. This is especially true if sexual intimacy is indeed a part of the relationship. For this reason, it is usually advisable to avoid passionate displays of affection in front of adolescents who are attempting to deal with their own sexual thoughts and feelings. At the same time, caring and affection for a partner can provide a model for the teenager to use in building future relationships with the opposite sex.

Teenagers have many conflicting moral codes to deal with today. Even though they are aware of the many differing values, teenagers are often very moralistic when it comes to their own parents' lives. They judge parental behavior in absolute right-or-wrong terms. They expect their parents to behave according to a strict moral code, and they can become extremely emotionally upset if they are somehow forced to acknowledge their parents' sexuality. Treating your adolescent's feelings with respect and being discreet about your sexual involvements may help to prevent angry scenes and emotional withdrawal by your adolescent.

Meeting your partner's children

Very often men and women who are planning to be married tell us they are about to meet their partner's children for the first time and are very nervous about how to handle this upcoming event. Often they have rehearsed in their minds what they are going to do or what may happen: "I'm going to walk right up to Johnnie and have a man-to-man talk with him." "I'm going to buy them all presents so I'll be able to let them know how glad I am to meet them." "I'm scared I won't think of anything to say and we'll just stand there and look at each other." "Maybe when she sees me she'll run away and hide."

It is certainly easier to get to know your stepchildren-to-be over a period of time while you and their parent are also getting to know one another. However, this is not always possible because the children may be with their other parent miles away from where you live. And so the anxieties about this first meeting build up on both sides.

The most important thing to remember is that relationships take time to develop. Children seem to be more aware of this than adults, for we've heard a number of stepchildren say that their parents seem to expect all concerned to get together and relate warmly as though they'd known each other for a long time "and that's not the way things work." Expecting that you and your stepchild or stepchildren-to-be will magically become friends in a moment or a day of being together can lead to nothing but disappointment, hurt feelings, and pressure for everyone.

Almost every adult has had the experience of visiting a friend who has children where it takes time to establish any contact and feeling of friendliness. If your friend's child is young, when you approach and try to make contact the child may back away, hide behind a chair, or run out of the room. However, if you say "Hi" and smile, and then sit down and begin talking to your friend, slowly the little child approaches. As more trust develops, he or she may begin to show you some favorite toys. Soon you have the beginning of a friendship and next time you will not have to wait so long for your friend's child to relate to you.

Older children also need to feel that they can approach and become involved with a new adult as they feel comfortable in doing so. There does not need to be any hurry. If you "come on strong," you may be rejected as "phony." After all, you have just met one another—how can you know the areas of life you will enjoy sharing?

Another pressure may be felt if you are the parent who is about to be remarried and your new partner is meeting your children for the first time. You want everyone to make a good impression. In fact, you're scared that the children will be rude, or silly, or somehow reflect badly on you as a parent. You also want your children to like the person whom you are going to marry. Do your best to relax. Plan something interesting to do such as going out to get ice cream cones or going to the zoo to feed the animals. In this way the new acquaintances will not need to say much to each other. Whatever you plan, make it a short visit, knowing that you will all have many times together in the future. It is difficult to be patient, but relationships can't be forced. Take your time—it is worth it. Trust between people needs to grow, and pushing for trust can often destroy the very thing you are wishing and hoping to develop.

3 | Remarriage Planning

Sharing expectations

Most of your marriage expectations come from the family you have
grown up in—you want your family to be like that family, or you want
it *not* to be like that family, or you want it to be like your next-door
neighbor's family, or a friend's family. If you have been married
before, you may have been disappointed after your first marriage did
not live up to your earlier expectations. After you've had that unfortunate experience, you may be expecting this *new* remarriage family to
be the family you've always dreamed about.

Since there are two adults with different past families and different
expectations, you may be on a collision course if you don't sit down together and think and talk about your ideas and expectations. For many
couples it is helpful to write them down. This makes it easier to see
where your ideas fit together well and where they don't fit together. If

you keep in mind that ways of doing things are not right or wrong but just different, then you can more easily work out compromises around your conflicting ideas and expectations.

Because at least one of you has been married before, you will, as we pointed out in Chapter 1, have expectations and ideas about how you want things to be done that come from a number of previous households—not just from the family you grew up in. It is important in any marriage to talk together about expectations, but it takes even more patience and understanding to do this when you have been married before because there will be many more people involved in your new household and you have ideas coming from a number of different places—your previous marriage family, your single-parent household, and the original family you knew as a child.

If you do write lists, they might look something like this:

Ellen's list	*Bob's list*
1. I want to continue with my present job.	1. I'll take care of the yard and fix the things in the house that break down.
2. I'd like help around the house from Bob.	2. I'd like to take care of paying the bills.
3. I don't want to take care of the bills.	3. I want to spend some time on the weekend watching sports programs on television.
4. I want Bob and me to go to the movies or do something alone each week, no matter whose children are here.	4. I'd like Ellen and me to go away together without the kids for a day or two each month.
5. No television for the children during the school week.	5. I expect Ellen's children to do their share around the place.
6. When Bob's children are with us, they have to help too.	6. There's no television for the children until all their homework is done.
7. I want to have a bank account of my own as well as a joint account.	

These lists have some of the bigger expectations on them, and may bring up questions that neither of you has ever considered. How does Bob feel about Ellen's continuing to work? How will the major home responsibilities be shared? How does Ellen feel about Bob's interest in sports? We find that very often partners planning to remarry have only "dated" and have never really talked about these day-to-day concerns. Often, when they get married, they feel disappointed, let down and angry because their expectations were so different. Each person had assumed that what he or she was expecting was what the other was also expecting.

It is easy to think there is a "perfect" solution for sticky spots where you feel differently. Sometimes this is true, but usually there is only a "best" solution, not a perfect one. There seems to be a difference in Ellen and Bob's expectations about what Bob is going to do inside the house—when the washer breaks, the toilet gets plugged up, and the lights burn out, Bob expects to take care of the repairs. However, things like this don't happen every day (hopefully). Ellen expects Bob to help vacuum and do the kitchen clean-up. Vacuuming occurs regularly and kitchen chores are daily. There are many alternatives to be considered, and perhaps tried, but none will give both Ellen and Bob 100 percent of what they said they wanted. Perhaps Bob will agree to take turns with Ellen doing the vacuuming, or Ellen will agree to work with the children at cleaning up the kitchen while Bob takes full responsibility for the vacuuming, or Bob and Ellen will hire someone to do the major house chores. There are a number of different solutions available, as long as you don't get stuck fighting over whose idea is "right" and start going around and around in angry circles.

A crucial but difficult area to work out together in remarriages has to do with expectations you have of your children and stepchildren. You feel differently about the children you've known from birth, with their dirty diapers, runny noses, and their loving smiles and warm hugs, than you do about stepchildren who don't even "feel" right when you touch them. At first, you and your future spouse might work together on very fundamental and simple expectations of the children—the television rules and a division of chores, for example. If you try to work out complicated mealtime rituals, food preferences, ways of dressing, "polite" conversational style, and the "refinements" of living, there seems no way to avoid hours of struggle. Stepchildren simply do *not* act the same as the children you've raised in actuality or in your fantasies.

One reason for concentrating on a few basic regulations is that jealousies among stepsiblings, as well as anger between adults, can arise easily if all the children are not expected to follow the same house rules. Having this happen is more difficult for the adults to manage than you may think.

Clarke and Sonia had difficulty in this area. They each had two children from previous marriages and they and the four children agreed that as far as the children were concerned:

1. Homework would be done right after supper before any TV watching.
2. The four children would do the supper dishes, switching specific chores each week (e.g., washing, drying, clearing the table, putting the dishes away).
3. Bedrooms would be left tidy or, if not, the doors would be kept closed.
4. On Saturday morning the bedrooms would pass inspection after the beds had been changed.

For a few weeks there was good cooperation, and then Sonia and Clarke began to argue because Clarke's son Tim developed headaches or stomachaches soon after dinner and also very often on Saturday mornings. Clarke was concerned and allowed Tim to watch TV while the other three did the evening clean-up, and Clarke helped Tim change his bed and clean his section of the boys' bedroom on Saturday morning.

Sonia, observing that Tim would recover rapidly so that he roughhoused with his stepbrother many evenings before bedtime and spent Saturday afternoon racing around the neighborhood with his friends, let Clarke know that she felt Tim was taking advantage of the situation. The other children also noted Tim's behavior and got angry and jealous of the special help Tim's Dad gave him. The children began to bicker with each other. Sonia and Clarke also began to argue more and more. As Clarke said, "I know my son wouldn't shirk on a job. He simply doesn't feel well. We'll take him to see the doctor." The pediatrician, however, could find nothing wrong with Tim, which fanned Sonia's anger and also the resentment of the other children.

After the visit to the doctor, Clarke began to ignore his son's complaints, even though he found it difficult to do so. Often Clarke had to find something to concentrate on for himself so he could withstand

Tim's whimpering. Almost miraculously, so it seemed to Clarke, Tim's health no longer was an issue, he did his share of the work, and abided by the homework rule. Sonia relaxed, most of the fighting between the children stopped, and the household started functioning in as smooth a manner as could be expected with four active children within its walls.

Moving slowly toward the remarriage

There are fewer people involved in a first marriage than in a remarriage, and the feelings are less complicated. In a first marriage mothers and fathers may be sad or glad to see their children getting married, and the partners themselves may feel scared and excited. Remarriages when there are stepchildren, by comparison, are complicated logistical emotional events. Your children or stepchildren-to-be are probably wondering where they're going to fit into the new scheme of things, your parents may be angry about your plans and worried that they'll not see as much of their grandchildren as before, and your ex-spouse may be upset and concerned that you'll want custody and visitation changes.

Taking time for all these people to get used to the changes that will take place calms a lot of fears. It also means that there will be fewer surprises for you, since all of the people who will be together at least part-time in the household will have a chance to know each other better. Pleasant surprises are great, but finding out that your new wife prefers her career to child-rearing, or prefers child-rearing to her career, when you'd counted on the opposite priority, is a difficult adjustment to face along with a myriad of other changes that are inevitable when people marry.

Following a divorce or death, your children had to deal with many changes which they couldn't control. To them the whole of life may have seemed unpredictable and changing every day. Moving slowly and letting your children help you plan ahead can ease their sense of helplessness so that they will be better able to handle the changes that will come along with your remarriage—a new adult, new children, new friends, a new school, a new home. If they feel happy about your remarriage it will certainly make things a lot easier for everyone.

To you it may feel as though you and your new partner have been together for a long time, but to your children, your parents, your former in-laws (your children's grandparents) and your friends it may seem as though it was only yesterday that you were paired with a different person. They have not been with you as you went for coffee together, went to the beach or the movies, or spent time alone at home. If at all possible give the important people in your life time to become familiar with each other and to feel some trust in the new relationships.

Possible custody and visitation changes

Many long-standing custody and visitation arrangements are altered after the remarriage of a parent. One new stepmother with a wry little smile put it this way, "My stepchildren were given to me as a wedding present by his angry ex-wife."

All too often couples marry without discussing the possibility that the children of one of them, or both of them, may come to live with them. Perhaps your children are living with your ex-spouse nearby or even in another state. You have no reason to consider that your former spouse will want the children to live with you, or you have a suspicion deep down that there is that remote possibility but it seems too complicating and upsetting to discuss with your new partner. So for many reasons you and your partner don't discuss the subject of children joining your household unexpectedly. However, many changes can occur and, because the children are members of two different households or at least have biological parents in two different households, there are more "housing" options open than in biological families. Because of this, changes in living arrangements often come up in the following situations:

- The parent with whom the children live becomes ill and can no longer care for them.
- The parent with whom the children live decides that the children would be "better off" in the new stepfamily.
- The children, particularly teenagers, decide that the new stepfamily household is where they want to live.
- A single parent feels overburdened or angry and leaves the children on the doorstep, suitcase in hand.

- A remarried parent finds that having a "home" again reawakens the desire to have his or her children live there or at least visit more frequently.

If your remarriage has taken place with no awareness or discussion on your part that children in such instances often do change residence, then it can be very difficult to discuss the matter amicably while a child waits on the doorstep!

Where to live?

It is difficult to have a new person or persons move into your "space" and it is difficult to be the "new" person or people joining a preexisting group. It helps cut down on feelings involved with "territory" if you are able to start out in a new place of your own.

Let's say you have two children and you have been living in a home with three bedrooms. You are marrying a person with no children. That sounds easy—after all, your partner will be in the bedroom with you, and the children will continue to have their own rooms as before. But your children have been used to free run of the house, including your bedroom. If this continues after you marry, then your new spouse is the only one in "unfamiliar territory." He or she may have difficulty feeling part of the household and may feel the lack of privacy or of time alone with you. In addition, your children may resent their new stepparent for intruding into what they considered their space. If you now make your bedroom "off limits" to your children, they may feel shut out and abandoned by you because of this new person. You feel caught in the middle as resentment slowly, or not so slowly, builds up between your children and your new spouse.

It is difficult to have a new person or persons move into your "space," and it is difficult to be the "new" person or people joining a preexisting group. For these reasons it helps to cut down feelings involved with "territory" if stepfamilies can start out in their own house or apartment.

For Lila and Fred the situation was different. They both had two children and because it made economic sense they decided to move into Fred's home, where he had continued to live after his divorce. The house had three bedrooms, and his children who lived with their mother still used their old rooms whenever they were with their father. That meant that when Lila and her children moved in, Fred's children's rooms became Lila's children's rooms, which were then "shared" with Fred's children when they were there. Fred's children felt betrayed by their father and displaced by Lila's children, and to them it felt like it all happened because of Lila. So whenever Fred's children were with Lila and Fred, his children were angry and upset, said nasty things to Lila, and fought with her children. Lila tried very hard to do nice things for all the children, but she soon felt unappreciated and angry. Fred, caught in the middle, felt guilty and angry. The children couldn't stand each other, and the entire household was in an uproar. New shared space, of course, doesn't solve everything, but it can help.

New partners are particularly likely to move into "old territory" when a former spouse has died. Many a new wife has moved into her husband's home to find life-size portraits of his former wife are still hanging in the front hall, and her cosmetics still in the dressing-table drawers. Throwing the cosmetics in the garbage and taking the pictures down seems sacrilegious to the children whose parent has died, while leaving the portraits around perpetuates the new wife's feeling that there's a ghost in the house. The past keeps intruding on the present.

Sometimes, it is impossible to buy a new house or change apartments. If you move into your spouse's house and knock out two walls, repaper all the rooms, and buy new furniture, it can feel a lot more like "your" home. However, many remarried women say that they experienced a tremendous sense of relief and joy when the family eventually bought or rented a house of their own, even though they had totally redecorated the old house. You cannot put a price tag on the good feelings and better relationships that result from finding a spot of your own to create together new stepfamily surroundings and traditions.

Space can be a problem in any kind of family. In a stepfamily, where you are bringing together people who have not grown up together, space is even more critical. Just imagine ten-year-old Jean's rage at having to share her room with four-year-old Nancy whom she doesn't really know and who has wrecked her panda bear collection, or Donald's feelings when he finds himself "assigned" to a tiny attic bedroom in the new house while his new stepbrother has the large bedroom right next to the bathroom they share.

Money can take care of space problems, but with child support going out, and perhaps alimony as well, and extra children to clothe and feed, stepfamilies as a group are not overly wealthy! Indeed, money is a very touchy area for stepfamilies. There are, however, a few helpful guidelines:

1. Consider it money well spent and the easing of many unpleasant hours if you can find a new living place to start your life together.
2. Include your children and stepchildren, whether they "visit" or live with you, in your search so that it will begin to be a "family" project from the start.
3. When it is time to decide who gets what space, have a family conference around this question. If the children are given the opportunity to help with this important part of the planning, they often come up with very creative ideas and are much more willing to negotiate than if they have no input on the subject. This is particularly important with older children, since they have more previous "family history" and expectations than the younger children.

   If you are not able to discuss the living arrangements together in a productive manner (see "Family Meetings" in Chapter 4), try asking a facilitator or moderator, such as a good friend, counselor, or family doctor, to help you.
4. When you move in, have all stepfamily members take part in the moving if at all possible.

Grandparents and stepgrandparents

Many brides and grooms the second time around are saddened because of the angry reactions of their parents. If you have never been married before and are marrying a person with children, your parents may have difficulty changing the picture in their heads of what your marriage was going to be like. They also are giving up cherished dreams about the way things were going to take place when you got married. If you are the bride, your mother and father may be upset that you are sharing this special day with stepchildren and express worry about "all the responsibility" you are taking on. Parents of the groom also worry about the added responsibility, so if you are a man who has not been married previously, or at least has no children from a previous marriage, your parents may be angry at the financial and parenting expectations they feel are being placed on you immediately.

One new stepgrandfather talked of the awkwardness and "squeamishness" he felt when one of the four stepchildren he had acquired that very day rushed to him and called him "grandpa." He'd not yet had any grandchildren, and he was overwhelmed at suddenly having four little ones under foot. He wondered where they were going to fit into the family tree, and besides, he just wasn't old enough to have a seven-year-old grandson!

It is hard not to feel extremely hurt when your excitement and anticipation are not shared by your parents, but if you realize that they are having to sort out even more than the usual mixture of feelings that accompany a first marriage for their child, you can perhaps understand your parents' reactions a little better. During your years of growing up your parents had not expected you to bring home a person with three children and say "We're going to be married."

Wedding plans

Modern weddings come in many sizes and shapes—in the air, under the sea, in a traditional church, in a beautiful park. The words said, the promises made, and the ceremonies themselves are as varied as the couples being married. In a marriage with children from a previous marriage, however, the cast of characters introduces complexity, not only because there are more central figures, but also because of the wide range of emotions often being experienced. You and your partner may be floating on a pink cloud while your children or stepchildren are excited, scared, angry, confused, or just feeling numb and very removed from it all. If you talk with the children you may find that they have the following questions and concerns:

- Will they continue to see their other biological parent as often as before the wedding?

- Will they have more or less time alone with the parent getting re-married?
- This wedding means that their two biological parents won't be getting back together again the way they'd kept dreaming.
- How can they ever live in the same house with so many other people they don't really know or like very much?
- Will their new stepparent play with them so they can all have a lot of fun together?
- How will they get to scouts next week, to ballet class on Thursday, to see their friends from their former school?
- The divorce was bad enough and now all this upheaval again. It isn't fair.
- How will Boots the cat and Rusty the dog get along together, and who is going to feed them?

Answering your children's questions, reassuring them whenever you can, and planning ahead so that everyone knows exactly what is going to happen can do a great deal to help them to calm down. Thinking about having a stepparent to play with and talk to makes some children happy, but for many others the fact that they will have to share a parent with a stepparent means they are losing someone again. You may need to stop Jimmie from tearing the house apart because he's confused and angry, but he may find it reassuring if you let him know that you understand how he feels, tell him what the plans for him are, give him a hug and send him out to play.

Including the children in the wedding service

Children who are very familiar with their stepparent-to-be often in-clude themselves in the scene, asking, "When is Harry going to marry us?" Perhaps your children are in this frame of mind and want to take an active part in your wedding ceremony. In such a situation, you can all enjoy planning how you want it to be. Depending on their ages, the children may be part of the wedding party as flower girl, attendant, usher, or simply in a part of the service—be it a large formal wedding or a family group in your own garden.

Many times older children, in particular, do not wish to take an active part in the service, and if you apply pressure of any kind they may refuse to attend at all or spread a truckload of gloom around if forced to be present. If your older children or stepchildren are reluctant to be there when you are married, but know that you will welcome them if they do decide to attend, very often they will decide at the last minute to join the festivities. But getting into a power struggle over whether or not they will be at the wedding launches the new stepfamily into a sea of acrimony rather than matrimony.

Unless you and your new partner have an exceptionally good relationship with your ex-spouse, it is unwise to count on his or her cooperation regarding your remarriage. Even if your ex-spouse was the one who wanted the divorce, your remarriage can stir up a confusion of feelings for him or her, particularly if you are the first to remarry.

In addition, bringing a stepparent into your household can give your ex-spouse, remarried or not, the feeling that he or she now has a "rival" for the children's affection. Therefore, it is better to take care of the arrangements yourself in regard to what your children will wear, how they will get to the ceremony, and any other details involving them.

Very often, in marriages involving children, the children stand next to or behind the couple during the service and the words of the service or the promises made include the children. For example, you may promise to care for your spouse's children or to do your best to help the children grow to be happy, loving adults. Unless the children are consulted and freely agree to take an active part in the service in terms of making promises of their own, it seems best to leave such words to the adults, since the adults, not the children, have made the decision to be married! If the children make promises which later are difficult to keep, their sense of guilt at failing to live up to their word may become an added burden for them.

If your children or stepchildren are not present at your wedding, it is somewhat more difficult for them to grasp the new reality, since rituals are concrete guideposts along the roads of life that help those involved recognize where they are. For your children, being present at your remarriage marks in a symbolic way the fact that new relationships and commitments now exist. It can make the new family seem more "real."

4 | The First Months

The nitty-gritty of daily living

Very often, after the marriage ceremony has taken place and parents and children are together under the same roof all of the time or for various lengths of time depending on custody and "visitation" arrangements, tensions immediately arise. As one individual commented, "The trouble with life is it's daily!"

Before the marriage there may have been an "end" to being together and therefore many little annoyances were overlooked. But now that there is a permanence about the venture, the fact that Ricky leaves his clothes all over the floor and Jill bangs the door whenever she has an opportunity may send shivers of discontent and then anger up your spine. What's more, their parent, your new spouse, isn't doing anything about it—and you don't understand why. In fact, your spouse

48

may not even notice the behavior you find so irritating, since that's the way it has always been in the previous household. If you have children yourself and talk with your partner about your upset feelings at Jill's and Rick's behavior, you may find that your partner has similar feelings about things your children do. "You get used to your own children's misbehavior patterns," as one father/stepfather put it. However, it is very important for you to talk together about what gets on your nerves, so you can *slowly* begin to work out new ways for this new household.

The children also may feel that things are not being done in familiar ways. Everyone in the household may be on edge, feeling awkward and strange, and not knowing what to expect. And there can be many surprises! It's great when they are happy surprises, and it's not so great when the surprises are upsetting. We have found that one of the most difficult things adults have to deal with after a remarriage is the expectation that their new household will operate smoothly from the first. Of course, the reason this can't happen is because everyone has walked into this new household with very, very different family experiences and ways of doing things.

No two people do things the same way, but people who grow up together do things more similarly than people who do not grow up together. Most of the time you're not even aware of how you take off your shoes, stir your coffee, use your fork, talk on the telephone, wash the dishes, fold the laundry, cook scrambled eggs, drive the car, brush your teeth, or close the door. Then put together under the same roof

---

Flexibility is the name of the game! It is likely that the children are more flexible than the adults. Adults have been forming their ideas of how to do things and how things "ought" to be done over a period of many years. In stepfamilies with their hazy boundaries, the comings and goings of the children, and the multitude of differences that exist, it is important to be flexible and shift with the constant alterations and changes. Change can be enriching and exciting if it is not met with resistance and fear.

people who do all these little daily tasks differently, and suddenly the differences scream at you! If you have been taught to eat bacon with a fork, and have taught your children to eat bacon with a fork—and there you are at breakfast with stepchildren who grab bacon off the plate and eat it with their fingers—something feels wrong. Each person in the family has experienced a number of different families with their individual ways of doing things before all of you got together, and for everyone, children and adults alike, the differences in the ways you all do things can seem mighty peculiar—and definitely wrong. To outsiders such differences may seem trivial, but unconscious emotional beliefs in how to do things are being challenged every minute of every hour! Major differences usually have to do with "discipline." This is discussed later in the chapter.

Many times in this situation one or both of the adults starts trying to "change" the children, or the children say, "Ugh, that's not the way my real Dad does it," or the spouses fight over how the dog's food is to be fixed, and which toothpaste will protect against cavities. In first marriages, couples have fewer differences to work out and more time in which to do it. As a new stepparent or remarried parent, give yourself time to work out how your new household is going to operate and be prepared to compromise. For a while, at least, you may be a two-toothpaste family.

Reactions of preschool children

Preschool children react strongly to the feelings and behavior of the adults around them. You need to tell them in language they can understand what is going to be happening in their lives for the next few days or weeks. If your children are very young, you will need to talk with them repeatedly about plans, because they cannot understand time yet and so are able to comprehend only one or two days at a time. When they are four or five, they may want to know the plans for the next week. The more routine the plans, the easier it is for preschool children. For example, if you tell Charlie that he will usually be with his mother and stepfather on days when he's not at nursery school and with you the days that he goes to nursery school, then he will feel calmer about what is going to happen, even if you have to keep reminding him. It can be very reassuring if you color in the days in two separate colors on a special calendar to let young children know which household they will be in on each day.

If you seem pleased with the arrangements, then your preschoolers are able to accept the plans much more readily and happily than if they sense that you are unhappy. Sometimes young children will cry and cling to you when they are going to their other household, especially if they feel that you are going to be either sad and lonely without them or angry if they have a good time when they are not with you. They love you and want you to be happy. If you can let them know you are happy when you are all together and also happy doing other things when they are not there, then your children can feel freer to come and go and not feel guilty that they are doing something that makes you unhappy. As a result, they may not cling and cry as they might otherwise.

In biological families, young children often cling and cry when they go to nursery school or kindergarten. As long as the parents accept this as a sign of insecurity which will soon disappear, the behavior usually is gone before you know it. In stepfamilies, the crying and clinging may indicate the types of anxiety just mentioned. However, instead of accepting the behavior calmly, the adults in stepfamilies often see the clinging as a signal for a change of custody or a complete rearrangement of the parent's or the child's life. Except in rare situations where a child may indeed be mistreated in one household, such behavior is no more serious than in other types of families. Doing something about custody changes at such times may have more to do with the feelings of the adults—guilt, anger, loneliness—than with the feelings of the child.

Preschoolers whose parents and stepparents are able to cooperate in planning for the children often move back and forth easily between their two households. They enjoy special times with both families and think that this is just the way the world is! Later on, when they are in school, they begin to learn, as do the other children, that there are many different family patterns and many different household rules and expectations.

Often five- and six-year-olds feel angry and confused at the time of the death of a parent or the divorce of their parents, particularly if they are not told what is happening. If you find it too hard to talk to your children about what has happened to change their lives, get a friend to help you talk with them. Otherwise, they may continue to feel confused and angry and expect that somehow things will go back the way they were before—and then when that doesn't happen, you may have a cranky, disobedient, or clinging little child on your hands. Young children have a hard time understanding what "getting divorced" really means; sometimes "getting *un*married" makes more sense to them. So it may be easier to talk about being "unmarried" and explaining that this change is only between the adults. Both adults are still parents to their children—this is not changed.

There is a book called *"Divorce Is . . . A Kid's Coloring Book"* that can be helpful for older preschoolers, as well as for school-aged children. This coloring book, with a special written message to parents, illustrates special areas of concern to children, including dating and remarriage. Reading and coloring a book like this together with your child may help in discussing what is happening. Children are resilient and can adjust to changes if it is made clear to them what is happening and what they can count on.

Reactions of children six to twelve years

Children of any age are confused if it is not clear to them what is going on around them—they can feel the "vibes" if something is upsetting or changing. Just as with younger children, older children need to be told about the plans that affect them—for example, if and when they will be moving to a new home or a new school, or when they will be with their other parent. Children continue to wonder about why their parents were divorced even after one or both have remarried. Even if they don't ask questions about it, they are often willing to listen if you talk with them about your divorce. They don't want the "gory details," as one youngster put it, but simple statements such as, "Mommy and I got married to each other when we were very young, and we thought we knew each other very well, but then we have found a lot of things that we don't agree on. We talked about them, but just couldn't feel okay, and so we kept arguing a lot and don't love each other any more. And now it's really good to have a new wife I know so well and love a lot."

It is important to make it very clear that when you are angry with your children it does not mean you don't love them, and that if you argue with them you are not going to divorce them—they are part of you and will always be your children. They also need to know that it is not *their* behavior that caused your divorce.

There are several books that can be helpful for children of this age. By reading and discussing these books with your children, you will give them the chance to bring up questions they may have. Teenagers often get a great deal of comfort for themselves in reading them to their younger siblings or stepsiblings. We suggest that you consult Appendix B, "Helpful Books," or write to the Stepfamily Association of America for a list of books that are available through them, or check out your local library.

A very important thing to remember is that your children are feeling as though an earthquake has struck their life. It is important to reestablish their confidence and sense of security by making plans and promises that can be carried out. In this way, the children begin to feel that the ground under their feet is becoming stable again. Of course, illness or some very unexpected event can cause a change of plans, but if there has been a stable pattern worked out, children can understand a necessary change of plans.

People do not like the feeling of helplessness, but everyone reacts to this emotion in different ways. In remarriage families, children in the six to twelve age group often hang on to the belief that they caused the original breakup and work hard to get their biological parents back together again. This is their way of saying to themselves, "See, I'm not really helpless." Sometimes their behavior may be annoying or downright obnoxious—being surly and "sassy," particularly to stepparents, fighting with other children, refusing to do what is asked at home or at school, breaking into tears over "nothing" or acting in just the opposite way by becoming an overly obedient, compliant, "good" child.

We believe there are three important things that parents and stepparents can do to help children through this period:

1. Let them know that you understand how upsetting it is to have so many changes about which they have no say going on in their lives. At the same time, you may need to help them to control the behavior they are displaying. Feelings and behavior are two sep-

arate things, and it is the *behavior*, not the *feelings*, that must be controlled. The feelings need to be brought out into the open and accepted by the adult—then the child will feel relieved and under less pressure to behave in upsetting ways.

2. Help your children find nondestructive ways to express the physical and emotional energy caused by angry feelings—for example, banging nails into a block of wood, punching a punching bag or pillow, running to the street corner and back three times.

3. Give the children as many choices as possible for different aspects of their lives. Choosing what they want to wear to school, what they want to eat for breakfast, how they are going to spend their allowance, what friends they want to play with, when they want to take a bath—all these and other choices help your children see that they do have control over many aspects of their lives. This can reduce their efforts to exert control by continually saying, "No, I won't!", being totally uncooperative, or acting out the role of the perfect, compliant child.

One eight-year-old, Rolly, dragged his way to school every morning, didn't get out of bed when asked, didn't get dressed in time for a good breakfast, wouldn't eat what was on the table, and finally slouched out to the bus stop just in time to climb aboard as his friends called to him to hurry. Then his father and stepmother changed a major aspect of the morning routine: Rolly had the choice of a variety of foods he could have for breakfast and could choose what he wanted in his lunchpail for his noon meal at school. Now Rolly sailed out of bed and dressed quickly so there was time to decide on his cereal and egg, or fruit and toast for breakfast, and also choose which juice and fruit, sandwich or cookie he wanted to find when he opened his lunch later. Children in all types of families need to have control over suitable aspects of their lives; for children who are adjusting to so many changes over which they have no control, a sense of mastery is extremely important.

Teenage children

Teenagers are learning to break away from the family unit as they "try their wings." Their bodies are changing and they are dealing with the emergence of sexual feelings. Their identity as individuals is in the process of formation. At the same time that they are turning more and more to their peer group for identity and support, they are also scared of leaving the security and familiarity they have had at home. So they go back and forth between wanting to be looked after and wanting to be independent.

As parents, you may also have mixed feelings, for you want your children to grow into independent, responsible adults, and at the same time you want to protect them from "making mistakes," getting into situations that were painful for you as you grew up, or doing things you feel are wrong.

In stepfamilies with teenagers, if the remarriage has taken place recently, teenagers often turn even more to their peer group for support and are reluctant to put out the effort to become part of the new household. As one 16-year-old said, "Two parents are too many! I don't need still another adult telling me what to do." And it makes no difference whether the new adult is strict or lenient, friendly or unfriendly—at this stage of their development, adolescents often "cut out of the household" a little faster than they might if there had not been a death or divorce and a remarriage. As in all types of families, they like to have the door left open so that they can return later as young adults ready to relate to family members in more adult relationships. Over and over again, grown stepchildren say to us that they really resented

Integrating a stepfamily that contains teenagers can be particularly difficult. At this age adolescents are moving away from their families in any type of family. In single-parent families teenagers have often been "young adults," and with the remarriage of a parent they may find it extremely difficult or impossible to return to being in a "child" position again.

Adolescents have more of a previous "family history" and so they ordinarily appreciate having considerable opportunity to be part of the stepfamily negotiations, although they may withdraw from both biological parents and not wish to be part of many of the "family" activities.

their parents and stepparents until they were on their own and then they formed warm and loving relationships with them later on. If older teenagers run out the door, this doesn't mean they are disappearing forever into the wild blue yonder!

The adults in stepfamilies often produce a lot of tension with teenagers because of their desire to have teenagers be fully participating members of the new household and their feeling that there are only a few more years to teach their values to the adolescents. Teenagers have spent more years than younger children living in a family or families with certain patterns. They are struggling to form their own identity, and while they can learn a lot (though you may not think they are even noticing) from the way the adults work together and how the stepparent does certain things differently, they usually fight any conscious efforts to discipline or change them.

Because of their age, it is particularly important to invite teenagers to contribute their ideas on how things might be done in the new household. Their sense of being in control, at least to some extent, over what is going on is very, very important to adolescents. As we have suggested before, see Appendix B or write to the Stepfamily Association of America for a brochure.

Stepparents with no children of their own

All of a sudden you are being faced with many complicated tasks. Not only are you having to adjust to being in a new partnership, but at the same time you are learning how to be a parental figure to children whom you have not raised "from scratch." The whole journey may appear to turn from an exciting adventure into a series of unexpected calamities. This usually happens because you are expecting the impossible of yourself and of the others in your household and there have been few guidelines or models to shape your expectations. Your stepfamily is different from the type of family you have learned about from your experiences while growing up. Here are some suggestions that may help you feel more comfortable with the new experiences you are having:

- Even though your spouse may have more practical knowledge or experience with children than you do, reading or taking a course together can be especially worthwhile.
- Talk to someone who is a stepparent or "knows the territory."
- Remember that everyone is feeling somewhat strange and that the children's feelings may be similar to the ones we have described — feelings which have little or nothing to do with the kind of person *you* are. You are not a failure as a stepparent simply because things are tense.
- Because your spouse has had a relationship with the children for some years, it will take you time to become a part of that group. Trying to blast your way in doesn't work but withdrawing and holding back won't get you into the group either.
- Your feelings about the children will probably be very different from those of your partner, since you are a stepparent and your partner is the parent. These differences in feelings may make it difficult for the two of you to understand one another with regard to the children. If this is a real problem for you, find someone whom you can talk with who understands and can give you the emotional support you need.

A study of this type of stepfamily points out that in most instances the stepparent needs to find support from friends, relatives, or a counselor outside of his or her immediate household. Of course, you hope you can get all the support you need from your new spouse, but the feelings are so different that it is not usually possible, even when there is a lot of love in your relationship.

- Make time for you and your spouse to be alone on a regular basis, to get away from family responsibilities; relax and concentrate on your couple relationship.
- Be as flexible as you can and give yourself the time it takes to work out satisfactory ways of being together.

Anne just *knew* she would be a good stepmother to her husband's three children since she had been an elementary school teacher for six years. She certainly was familiar with all the tricks children try to play and she had been very successful in handling discipline in her classes. At the same time, she let her students know she cared about them and was supportive of them. It had been a rewarding six years, and she loved children.

Anne and Jerry had been married for three months and things were not going as Anne had anticipated. Jerry's ex-wife telephoned frequently to discuss the problems she was having with Tina, Lisa and Robert. Anne felt excluded and cut off from Jerry during these conversations, and her irritation lasted for several hours. When the children came for the weekends, Anne had spent considerable time planning special projects which she knew children of their ages enjoyed. But Tina, Lisa and Robert were singularly unimpressed. No one wanted to put the special kites together. No one wanted to learn how to create the lovely folded paper animals and birds. No one wanted to mold clay figures that could be colored and preserved by heating in the oven. Jerry was very anxious to have Anne and his children love each other, and he tried to interest his children in what Anne and he had planned, but after a while he gave up in frustration and retired behind his newspaper. So once again Anne felt alone, and rejected as well. She became increasingly depressed as she swallowed her angry feelings and withdrew more and more from Jerry and from the children.

Communication between Jerry and Anne became as strained as between the adults and the children. Soon Lisa, Tina and Robert said they didn't want to come over on the weekends except occasionally. Jerry felt guilty and angry. Anne felt misunderstood, rejected and unappreciated.

Fortunately, Anne had a friend who belonged to a group of stepmothers who met once a week. She joined the group, and listening to the other women and sharing her problems with them turned the situation around for Anne, and then for the rest of the household:

- She found that her feelings were similar to others in the group, and so she relaxed and felt her sense of self-esteem begin to rise again.
- She realized that she had planned the weekends the way she planned her classroom activities, and had come on too strong in her attempts to move into the group.

- She stopped organizing the family, and Jerry and the children gradually began talking of things they liked to do; then Anne joined them in those activities.
- The three children began to come over more, which pleased both Jerry and Anne, and the warmth and caring between the couple grew strong again.
- The children began to approach Anne, Lisa more slowly than Tina and Robert, asking Anne to help them with special school projects and sometimes with their homework.
- Jerry felt comfortable with his new household, found that his telephone conversations with his ex-wife no longer seemed so necessary, and therefore the contacts became briefer and less frequent.

By learning from other stepmothers that she was encountering common stepfamily situations and emotions, Anne regained her sense of worth as a person. She relaxed and no longer felt she had to work hard to cultivate relationships. Instead, she let things grow more naturally and at their own pace. The tension and pressure in the household subsided and the abilities Anne had wanted to offer to the family became assets which were more valued when she allowed the children to approach when they were ready.

Remarried parents with no stepchildren

If you are a remarried parent married to someone who has no children of his or her own, you are neither learning to be a parent nor having to adjust to children not your own, but you are in the position of adding another person into your "group." While you can be very helpful to your new spouse by supporting him or her, you may create disharmony rather than harmony, if you carry a load of guilt and try to force a relationship between your new partner and your children. It will take your children time to form a relationship with your new spouse, and vice versa. Expecting stepparents and stepchildren to have caring feelings about each other right away can create a sense of pressure and resentment instead. You do need to make room for your spouse to join the group by including him or her in outings, games in the evening, or plans for the family. Through doing things together, relationships grow; however, to focus too much on the relationship and expect certain feeling responses immediately is like trying to pass laws about how people are going to feel. There is a law about school attendance, but just imagine the resentment if there were a law requiring that school teachers love their students and students love their teachers!

For one remarried father it was not enough that his wife came to nearly all the swim meets his children entered; she was supposed to *feel* the same way he did—exhilarated and excited. Until he could accept the fact that they felt differently, there was considerable tension between them.

As a remarried parent, you may be feeling pulled in many different directions by your new partner, your previous spouse, your children, and perhaps also your parents and former in-laws. One remarried father experiencing these feelings said, "I feel utterly helpless. I just want to have everyone be happy and have things run smoothly, but I can't find any way to make it work."

It is easy to see how you can be feeling helpless in such a situation, but you are actually in a powerful position, since you are the adult in the stepfamily who is a member of all the different subgroups; for example, you have a relationship with your spouse, a relationship with your children, and a relationship with your parents. This gives you the power to influence these different groups.

We will be talking about relationships with ex-spouses and grandparents later. At this point, during the early months of your marriage, the two most important groups to influence are the ones in your household—you and your partner, and you and your children (the group which has been together longest). Here are a few guidelines for using your power.

1. If you are supportive of your new spouse, the children will not be able to "divide and conquer."
2. Since your children are familiar with you and your rules, the household will run more smoothly if you continue to take a leading role in nurturing them and in setting limits.
3. To expect that you can keep everybody happy is setting yourself up for disappointment and feelings of failure. There are times of

unhappiness in all families, and during periods of transitions and new adjustments most people feel tension and stress.

4. Because you love both your spouse and your children, you may find it difficult to step back and let them slowly get acquainted with each other—laughing together, playing together, and arguing with each other. But if you don't "get out of the middle," you will continue to feel pulled apart and your children and their new stepparent will not have an opportunity to work out their own relationships.

Both adults are stepparents and parents

As you can see, there are many different types of stepfamilies, and while there are many similarities in all the different kinds, there are also certain differences. In the stepfamilies where both adults have children, remarriage is like the merging of two companies, each with its own president and employees, rules and regulations. At least each adult has had the similar experiences of being a parent and now relating to new children and of belonging to a parent-child group in the household as well as to a couple partnership.

If this is your type of stepfamily, you may find it easy at times to understand the feelings and reactions of your spouse. However, you may also find that each of you draws closer to your own children when you are having difficulty in your couple relationship. You have some support right within the household when things are not running smoothly.

The danger in this type of stepfamily, however, is that you may divide into two separate groups under the same roof—with an adult and related children in each of the two groups. The usual complaint is, "She expects my children to be perfect while her little darlings are allowed to do anything they please," or "He lets his children run wild, but let my Mary so much as leave her room a bit messy and he's yelling his head off at her."

You both have developed your own parenting styles and having your spouse criticize your children can feel like criticism of you. Also, you and your children have known each other and understand each other's little gestures, voice inflections, and ways of behaving. On the other hand, it is easy to misinterpret the actions and words of your stepchildren, particularly when you are feeling insecure and anxious. As soon as two different "groups" get together, each group is very conscious of how the others are relating to each other, especially since there have been no emotional attachments formed that can obscure and interfere with being objective about what is going on.

Stan and Shirley illustrate the need for couple unity to avoid the two-family-under-one-roof syndrome. Each adult brought three children to their marriage of one year's duration. Stan's children were in their late teens, and Shirley's were 11, 12, and 14. As can be imagined, it was instant chaos when they were all together and the custody/visitation arrangements put them together nearly half of the time. There was child support coming in from Shirley's ex-husband, but it was far from balancing the child support that Stan was paying to his ex-wife. This angered Stan and produced guilt in Shirley. However, the couple didn't really talk about money to each other and their feelings slipped indirectly into their conversations: "Shirley, your children never turn off any lights, and the other day I found Tommy had left the oven on all night! That costs a lot of money, you know." Then Shirley would withdraw behind her guilty shield, be depressed, and scold her son Tommy. At the same time, Shirley would defend Tommy to her husband, pointing out, "Stan, your children are no better. They buzz around in the car all the time and never think to put any gas in the tank. The other morning I was late to work because I had to stop for gas or I'd have been stranded on the freeway."

The children, sensing the chill in the air between the adults, wedged their way between the two, siding in subtle ways with their biological parent and putting down their stepparent. In fact, the rift widened and the older children began pushing harder as they started smoking pot in the house and staying out past 11 P.M. on school nights, against house rules. Finally Shirley's anger and despair were too much to contain. She insisted that everyone get together to talk. Stan resisted at first, but eventually joined the group as the gripes flew thick and fast.

The turning point came when Shirley began to cry and said she needed help from everyone, and maybe they all needed help working out of the chaos. Everyone felt hurt and misunderstood. Shirley and Stan came together as they talked directly about the family's budgetary problems, and slowly the entire group worked on ways to make the household work better—ways of saving on fuel costs, switching rooms so the "neat" boys shared a room and the "messy" ones could be messy behind closed doors, changing chores each week and putting the weekly list on the bulletin board for everyone to see. All agreed that car privileges and movie privileges would follow the successful completion of the weekly chores.

The "armed camps" dissolved in good humor as the group decided it was too late to do anything but go out to eat together. Shirley and Stan had learned a big lesson. In the future they promised each other they would talk together about bothersome situations, and once in a while the whole group would get together to work out any current difficulties.

Another stepfamily worked out their tensions and rough spots by having a special pot in which everyone could place a note about his or her gripes. When there were several slips of paper in the pot, all got together and discussed the issues—with suckers for the children at the bottom of the pot "to sweeten it," the adults said.

Still another stepfamily had two containers—one for complaints and one for things especially appreciated. When this family gathered together, they dealt with the problems first and then ended with a warm glow as they shared the little things and the larger happenings that had brought them pleasure during the past few days or weeks.

It is hard not to fight over differences or to avoid "straightening out" your spouse or your stepchildren. Try your best to be tolerant and give this new venture time. Everyone concerned needs to work out new roles and rules. It can be well worth the effort.

Discipline

From the first day in a stepfamily, you are faced with a need to define the limits of behavior and establish new disciplinary rules. In a biological family, on the other hand, there is a time of nurturance where the baby receives love and caring from the parents; then, ever so slowly, the parents begin setting limits as the child grows and explores so he or she will learn what is dangerous, what hurts other people and what just "doesn't go" in their particular family or neighborhood.

Not so for stepfamilies. There may be instant chaos as half-grown children push at the limits, battle against the changes thrust upon them and turn the household into a three-ring circus. Because there has not been a time of nurturance and bonding between stepparents and step-children before the need to discipline or set limits in the household, a new stepparent who comes in full of good intentions and tries to exert discipline often encounters difficulty. The stepchild has no real desire to please this new "unrelated" person, and so the stepparent may feel that the only way to get obedience is by utilizing force. But, as any book on discipline will tell you, you very shortly run out of power and end up feeling helpless, frustrated, defeated, and extremely angry.

Many stepparents expect to be able to discipline their stepchildren before building a friendly relationship with them. If you have this ex-pectation, it is probably leading to many difficulties not only with your stepchildren (unless they are very young), but also with your spouse, who feels your frustration and anger and rushes to defend his or her children.

Discipline is an issue in most families of any kind. There are many books written on the subject. If both adults will read one or more such books it can help you clarify and increase your skill in this area. A par-ticularly helpful book is *How to Discipline With Love* by Fitzhugh Dodson.

While *both* nurturance and limit-setting are important in all families for the development of independent, self-reliant adults, it is very com-plicated to provide both necessities in the early stages of a stepfamily. Even when there is agreement on parenting styles between the couple, studies of a number of stepfamilies all indicate that it usually takes a minimum of 18 months to two years for a stepparent to achieve an equal "co-management" role with the biological parent. This period of time is needed because it can take this long for a friendly or caring rela-tionship to develop between stepparents and stepchildren. Only when stepchildren wish to please their stepparents can they fully accept a limit-setting or disciplinary role on the part of the stepparent.

What, then, can you do about discipline during these early months, before a friendly relationship has developed?

1. As a stepparent, do not burden yourself with the unrealistic ex-pectation of riding in on a white charger to save the family from total chaos.

While discipline is not usually accepted by stepchildren until a friendly relationship has been established (often a matter of 18 to 24 months), both adults do need to support each other's authority in the household. The biological parent may be the primary disciplinarian initially, but when that person is unavailable it is often necessary for that parent to give a clear message to the children that the stepparent is acting as an "authority figure" for both adults in his or her absence.

Unity in the couple is important to the functioning of the stepfamily. When the spouses are comfortable with each other, differences between them in regards to the children can sometimes be worked out in the presence of the children, but at no time does it work out for either children or adults to let the children approach each adult separately and "divide and conquer." When disciplinary action is necessary, if it is not kept within the stepfamily household many resentful feelings can be generated. For example, if visitation rights are affected, the noncustodial parent is being included in the action without his or her representation. Such a punishment, then, may lead to difficulties greater than the original behavior that caused the disciplinary action.

2. Talk together as a couple and be supportive of the parent as this person enforces the rules with his or her own children. If there are two sets of children, the rules need to be the same for all and enforced by each parent for his or her own children.
3. Discuss your couple and parenting problems when you are alone—not in front of the children.
4. Concentrate on a maximum of three to five specific disciplinary areas important to both of you. If you try to remake the family too quickly, everyone will be confused and frustrated and a revolution may begin to brew.
5. The three to five disciplinary areas need to be specific. "We want Jim to shape up his manners" is not sufficiently descriptive. "We

want Jimmie to sit at the table with us during mealtime" is clear, easily understood and enforceable.

6. With everyone present, let your children know that when you are not with them their stepparent is acting in your stead to see that the family rules are carried out (as you might authorize a baby-sitter to enforce the rules when you are not going to be there).

7. As you build a relationship with your stepchildren, slowly begin to share the limit-setting role with your spouse.

8. Do not use disciplinary measures that will in some way affect the children's other household. As an example, do not restrict children's time with their other parent as a punishment for coming home an hour later than promised. Be sure the consequence stays in your own household—whether no TV for the next two days or whatever seems appropriate.

9. Details and examples are well presented in books dealing specifically with discipline; however, there are a few important guidelines to remember:

- When you want to change behavior, rewards and positive attention work better than negative attention and punishment.

- Negative attention is better than no attention at all from the child's point of view, so misbehavior may be an attempt to get through to you so that you will notice and pay attention to him or her.

- Make the consequences of undesirable behavior fall upon the person involved, not upon you as the adult and parent or stepparent. For example, make it clear that if bicycles are left in the driveway they may not be seen and may get run over by the car; if this happens, then it will be the bicycle owner's responsibility to replace the bicycle. Some chores may be made to enable the child to earn money to fix or replace the bike.

- Do not impose double consequences. For example, if a child is required to stay after school to finish an assignment, it would be a "double consequence" to then require that he or she work an extra half-hour at home. The discipline has already taken place at school between the teacher and the student. If you have agreed that the consequence of a messy room is that the bedroom door is to be kept closed, then it would be a double consequence (and also one requiring an additional enforcement effort on your part) if you nag and scold about the mess in the bedroom.

Feelings of frustration may come out very strongly in disciplining. As one stepmother said, "Because I can't control and get from my stepchildren what I want—their affection—I control what I can when I say, 'Go brush your teeth, wash your hands, make your bed.'"

Talking with other parents and stepparents can often help, though this is not always the case because there are so many different ideas about child-rearing and this often leads to feelings of confusion. This is why reading and taking parenting classes can be helpful in this particular area of family living.

If you are a stepparent, you may feel that you cannot let your stepchildren know your feelings when they leave your tools out in the rain, spill cranberry juice on the livingroom rug, or talk to you in an insulting manner. If you do not let them know that these behaviors are upsetting to you, your stepchildren may feel you simply don't care about them. They need to know what disturbs you. If they feel that nothing they do matters to you, then this can signal to them that you simply don't care about them. Interacting around these needs of yours is different from using a heavy hand in trying to remake a child or to suddenly change the way the family has been functioning.

Another trouble spot in connection with discipline is that you may feel that you discipline your children because you love them, but that your partner, as a stepparent, is disciplining them from anger and lack of caring. It may be reassuring for you to realize that fathers who were separated from their children for some months or years during wartime often returned home to the same disciplinary difficulties outlined in this chapter.

What children call their stepparents

It is difficult for adults to realize the importance to children of what they call their stepparents. One grown stepchild remarked that he and his stepmother got along beautifully for three years until the day she asked him to call her "Mother," while another 15-year-old boy said, "I asked if I could call him 'Dad' and he said, 'No.' It blew my mind. I was trying to accept him. It really hurt." A neighbor said, "There's no love in that house," because it was a stepfamily where the stepchildren had known their stepfather previously in another role and called him "Mr.

T." This was interpreted as a lack of caring and closeness, when the opposite was the case.

It seems to us that the basic rule is to talk names over with the children and follow their lead in what is comfortable for them. Stepparents generally call their stepchildren by their given name, such as Sally or Joe or Curt, which is what the children are called by relatives, friends, and neighbors and carries no relationship connotations. However, any derivative of "mother" or "father" refers to a relationship and thus may be fraught with emotional significance.

In their desire to present a close-knit family image or to feel part of the family, stepparents and parents often push for relationship terms such as "Mom" and "Dad," or "Mama" and "Papa," or straight "Mother" and "Father." For many children this creates distance and nonacceptance because they see these terms as symbolizing a replacement or loss of their other biological parent. Consequently, instead of unifying the stepfamily, it acts as a barrier to integration.

Other stepparents, in their awareness of the children's need to retain a relationship with their absent biological parent, may not allow a stepchild to use a name which is the same as or similar to that which the child calls the other parent, even though the child feels perfectly comfortable doing so. Children don't get confused over which "Grandma" it is, nor do some children feel confused over which "Mom" it is. Often children refer to a stepparent by his or her first name at home and as "Mother" or "Father" outside of the household.

In addition, the feelings of the absent biological parent are important to the child. When a stepparent is called "Mom" or "Dad," the other parent may feel as though he or she is losing the relationship with the child. One such parent said, in fear and anger, "He can't call her 'Mother'—he already has a mother!" Such an emotional reaction must be dealt with by the child. For all these reasons it is important to talk with your children and stepchildren about what they wish to call their stepparent because it often disturbs the children even though they may not bring it up for discussion.

Observation suggests that most stepchildren start out calling their stepparent by his or her first name, while many later on change to a relationship term. There are, however, many integrated stepfamilies in which the stepchildren continue to call their stepparent by his or her first name. In other words, at the present time there is no evidence to indicate that what a stepparent is called can be used to measure the quality of the relationship between the stepparent and stepchild; there is, on the other hand, observational and clinical evidence to suggest that, if adults are willing to let their children follow their own feelings, the steprelationship will flow more smoothly. Obviously, if the stepparent is uncomfortable at being called Mom or Dad and thus acknowledged as "related," or feels uncomfortable at *not* being acknowledged as a "family member" because the stepchild does not use a relationship term, emotional distance will be created. Hopefully, you will be comfortable with what your stepchild chooses to call you. What you are called does not measure what your relationship is or what it can become.

New traditions

Traditions bind groups together and provide anticipation, enjoyment, and warm memories. Members of a stepfamily come together with memories of traditions from former families. As you start your new stepfamily unit, you do not have shared memories or special rituals and ways of marking special occasions that are common to you all. You have little or no shared history. It is important to know the traditions of the families you all come from and then to share the new or combined ways you want to celebrate birthdays and special holidays, spend your vacations or share interesting activities together. Planning and working out these events create a unique set of traditions for your particular family, and these become the family history and memories for the future.

One stepfamily started a tradition on the first day of its existence as a unit. Each adult had children, and at the time of their marriage the couple gave each of the children a silver cup with the child's name and the date engraved on the cup. Now each child had something special and similar which marked for each a shared memory of an important day. Since that time, on special occasions these cups are used by the family and provide a tradition appreciated by all members of the family unit.

A teenager looking back remarked wistfully that she wished her stepfamily had done more fun things together. She said "I thought I was being selfish because I wanted to go places with my family, but I don't think so now. I think I just wanted us to be together. I wish I had more pleasant memories now." Going on picnics, walking on the beach, going out for hamburgers, going to the circus, seeing a movie together, or doing whatever pleases the members of your new stepfamily—these events, however small, create your shared stepfamily memories and history.

There are traditions of many kinds. One reason it is important to talk about past rituals before settling on new ones for your particular family is to prevent your children and stepchildren from feeling that there was something "wrong" with the way things were done before. If this had been done in eight-year-old Ann's new household, it is much less likely that she would have cried and then said, "We never celebrated Christmas that way before! We always opened our stocking presents before breakfast, and then had our presents after we ate. Now you say that's not the right way to do it!" There is no "right" or "wrong" way, but if the former "different" ways aren't part of the information that is shared in making your plans, your children may feel the way Ann did.

In planning celebrations you may have a little trouble pleasing everyone, but you may be surprised at the good ideas your children come up with—making candy together for Thanksgiving, decorating the house for Halloween with homemade figures of goblins and witches, playing Monopoly on certain weekends, doing a huge jigsaw puzzle which may take a number of weeks to finish, having a living Christmas tree or going to a tree farm to cut your own, having special birthday rituals for each person, going to certain baseball games. These are the ways that your family will develop its own uniqueness and its own sense of history.

New roles and new rules

Figuring out in a new group who is going to do what, and even what is going to be done, takes time and patience, compromise and negotiation. And stepfamilies need a lot of that!

Let's say you are a woman and find yourself and your eight- and ten-year-old daughters, as well as the girls' cat, living in a new home with your new husband, his three teenage children and their large German

Shepherd dog. The house is cluttered with furniture and toys, children are everywhere you turn, and dog hair sticks to you every time you stop to rest. You have decided to stay home and look after things and your husband has taken on a new job with long hours to help defray the extra expenses of this whole undertaking.

Before you were married, you and your children lived in a three-bedroom apartment, with maintenance included in the rent, and a gardener to care for the surrounding grounds. You worked hard as a nurse, but when you came home, after stopping on the way to pick up your children, supper and the evening went rather calmly. As for your husband, Charles, he had also lived in an apartment, with his parents nearby to keep an eye on the teenagers. As for Rover, he was used to having the run of the apartment and enjoyed snuggling up to everyone as close as his bigness would allow, leaving a trail of dog hair wherever he went. And TV dinners were the rule!

Children as well as adults in a stepfamily have a "family history." Suddenly these individuals come together and their sets of "givens" are questioned. Much is to be gained by coming together as a stepfamily unit to work out and develop new family patterns and traditions. Even when the individuals are able to recognize that patterns are not "right" or "wrong," it takes time and patience to work out satisfying new alternatives.

Values (the underlying approach to life and general ways of doing things) do not shift easily. Within a stepfamily different value systems are inevitable because of different previous family histories, and tolerance for these differences can help smooth the process of stepfamily integration. Needs (specific ways individuals relate together, individual preferences, etc.) can usually be negotiated more quickly than can general values. Having an appreciation for and an expectation of such difficulties can make for more flexibility and relaxation in the stepfamily unit. Negotiation and renegotiation are needed by most such families.

You are all going to need to do a lot of planning: Who will sleep where? Who will take care of Rover? Who will empty the trash or set the table? Where will you put your favorite reading lamp? Whose bathroom scales are expendable? Will the children be allowed to watch T.V. before doing homework? Which car will you drive to work?

You will undoubtedly need to decide together how to handle many similar situations. One way of doing this is for the adults to make a list of chores that need to be done to keep the family going—laundry, shopping, cooking, cleaning, dishes, paying bills, etc. This list will provide the starting point for a family meeting. To quote one teenager, "The adults need to talk and decide what they want and expect *together*—what they want from everybody—and then you all get together and talk. This is easier than trying to redesign rules as you go along. But don't have a dictator. Everyone needs to be involved."

The children may have other things to add: Who will pick them up after basketball practice? Who will bake or buy cookies for the monthly class bake sale? Who will make the special trip to the pet store for fish food? And on and on. The next step is to see if there are volunteers for any of the chores. In the stepfamily we have been talking about, one teenager volunteered to do the grocery shopping because then he was sure he'd have in the house what he wanted to eat; the 14-year-old volunteered to take care of Rover because she loved all animals and besides this was "her" dog; Charles volunteered to cook one night a week so his wife could attend a special class; and 16-year-old Amy somewhat reluctantly agreed that she'd prefer to cook than to do the dishes. Of course, there were items that had no takers and these needed to be assigned and rotated often. A chart posted in the kitchen helped to keep track of everything. Young children enjoy pasting gold stars on the chart when their chore is done. Older children like the same thing, or marking it off clearly with a brightly colored pencil. A collection of stars or check marks each week can bring a feeling of pride when noticed by a parent or stepparent!

Once jobs are chosen or assigned, you may need to compromise, at least during the first months, about *how* chores are completed. Your teenage stepdaughter may have learned to fold towels differently from the way you like them—criticizing her way of doing things will only cause resentment in the early stages of relationship-building. Your new husband may prefer to vacuum and then dust, while you consider it proper to dust and then vacuum. Such different ways of cleaning should certainly be tolerated. One 18-year-old kept putting the butter in the refrigerator when he cleared the table. He was repeatedly scolded by his stepfather who wanted it left out to stay soft. After seeing this scenario countless times, the boy's mother suddenly realized the problem: "For 12 years I trained my son to put the butter in the fridge. That's just the way he grew up." If you will keep in mind that it is the task that is important and not the way it is done and that members of your present family have learned a variety of "right" ways to do things, you will be able to work out over a period of time satisfactory methods of getting done what needs to be done in the new household.

Family meetings

Communication among stepfamily members is important. Family meetings are useful to plan fun times, as well as to hash out together the new roles and new rules for the household in the manner just suggested. They can also serve another function if adults and children are able to listen to one another as they talk about things that are bothering them. Occasionally, during the early months of a stepfamily, the presence of an outside person whom you like and trust may be necessary to facilitate the discussion, keep the emotions of the individuals under control and in perspective, and help each person listen to the others. Feelings must be stated without blaming or attacking other family members. The idea is to negotiate satisfactory solutions to situations as they arise.

There are several ways to set up family meetings:

1. There can be a box into which family members put their "grievances." A meeting is held when there are several slips in the box.
2. A regular time each week can be set aside as a time for all to get together and talk.
3. Any family member can request a family meeting.

There are certain rules that make family meetings work.

1. The feelings of every family member count equally, regardless of age.
2. Feelings are accepted and not judged as being right or wrong, valid or invalid, reasonable or unreasonable.
3. Accusations are not allowed. This means that people give what are called "I" messages rather than "You" messages. You really *are* talking about your own feelings and so it is more accurate to say, "When *I* came home last night and found the kitchen a mess, *I* felt angry and hurt and discouraged because no one had paid attention to my asking for the dirty dishes to be put in the sink." The alternative is provocative and inflammatory: "Nobody cares what happens around here. I came home last night and the kitchen was a mess. *You* are all really selfish and *you* are irresponsible." The first message, the "I" message, is heard better because the listeners are not feeling attacked and defensive.

    If you are interested in reading more about using this type of communication skill, the book *Children, the Challenge*, by Rudolph Dreikurs and Vicki Soltz is a good resource. And if you find that your "family meetings" become unproductive, "dumping" sessions, you may need to meet with a counselor to help you through tense and difficult times.
4. After the feelings have been expressed, there comes the problem-solving phase, followed by the formulation of the best possible solution which will meet the needs of the family members. During the problem-solving periods, the adults have a different function from the children in that they have had more experience and knowledge than the children and carry the financial responsibility for the family. Thus, practical considerations will sometimes make certain proposed solutions impossible to carry out.

    Try not to take more responsibility than you need to and thus carry a heavier load than necessary. One remarried couple spent several hours discussing and then arguing over how much allowance the two children should receive. The father of the 12-year-old girl felt that she should receive more money than her eight-year-old stepsister. The mother of the eight-year old girl felt that her daughter would think it was unfair if both children didn't receive the same amount. The discussion and argument went on and on. Finally they decided to have a family meeting and the four of them had the matter settled in less than 15 minutes. Both children agreed that the older one needed more money than the younger one, and therefore the allowances should not be the same amount!

5. End the meeting with positive and encouraging comments so that everyone can have a sense of accomplishment and good feelings. This produces warmth between the family members and an increase in each individual's self-esteem and sense of self-worth.

For family meetings, some families have discovered that what we call the "two container system" has worked well for them. The first container is for family members to use for notes about things that have not worked well and that need to be discussed. Together family members seek solutions, without blaming or anger. It helps to write a note for later discussion because you know it will receive attention and as a rule you will have had time for your feelings to calm down before the family meeting.

The other container is for positive comments about things that have gone well. Family members respond positively to being mentioned with appreciation for the considerate things they have said or done, and the family meeting can end on a positive note, both literally and figuratively. Everyone has an opportunity to feel good about what they are all accomplishing as they work together to form a satisfying new family unit.

5 | Forming New Relationships

In biological families, the new couple may spend a considerable amount of time alone, adjusting to one another, getting to know one another's likes and dislikes, working out ways of relating, and "building a nest" for themselves. And then, if they both so choose, the size of the family increases slowly. Even with these gradual changes, the birth of a child significantly alters the family pattern and new adjustments are necessary.

In stepfamilies there is a new couple and one or more children—often many more—all scrambling to make a myriad of adjustments to new roles and new relationships while dragging with them bits and pieces of former "nests."

The new couple relationship

There are many pulls, both internal and external, which make it difficult for a new couple to adjust easily and work together smoothly where children from previous marriages are also part of the picture.

If you and your spouse have had time alone before having any children come to live with you, you may have had an opportunity to adjust to one another's preferences—she knows what foods you like, that you need half an hour of silence in the morning before you can relate, and that you like to watch TV football games on Sunday afternoon; he knows that you want a cup of coffee first thing in the morning, are grumpy when you are hungry, and like a lot of affection.

However, even if you are lucky enough to have this "honeymoon" time together, there may be pulls from the past. Your children who are living with their other parent may call often and want contact, money, or an invitation to come to your new home; friends or relatives of one of you may keep talking about events that happened to one of you in the past, while the other feels left out and is silent; a former spouse may write to say that the property settlement and custody and visitation arrangements are not fair and must be changed immediately!

It is difficult to prevent the past from intruding into your present and making you feel angry or guilty—or both. And then you may turn from making love to constantly discussing and arguing about plans which never seem quite satisfactory. Soon you may find yourselves spending hours talking about whether or not to pay the extra orthodontic bill for a child, what amount of child support really is fair or when and how to arrange for Dick and Sally to be with you. Your pleas-

---

Parent-child relationships have preceded the new couple relationship. Because of this, many parents feel that it is a betrayal of the earlier parent-child bond to form a primary relationship with their new partner. A primary couple relationship, however, is usually crucial for the continuing existence of the stepfamily, and therefore is very important for the children as well as for the adults. A strong adult bond can protect the children from another family loss, and it also can provide the children with a positive model for their own eventual marriage relationship. The adults often need to arrange time alone to help nourish this important couple relationship.

ant times together are slipping away, replaced by frequent periods of anger and frustration.

You do need to talk to each other about these matters, but you also need to nourish your own couple relationship. It usually takes a lot of conscious effort to put aside matters that stir emotions of anger and hurt to turn to matters that feel warm and comfortable. Perhaps you can devise a plan something like this:

1. Decide together how much time each week will be productively spent in discussing matters pertaining to absent children and former spouses.
2. Pick the best time for the two of you to talk about these matters, and set a time limit on the discussion. New issues will always come up, so do not expect to settle everything once and for all.
3. Plan at the close of this discussion what time will be set aside to talk about these matters in the next two days, or weeks, or whatever interval works for you.
4. Remember that there *are* solutions, but not *perfect* solutions, and so don't keep disappointing yourselves by expecting to find simple or perfect answers.
5. Allow time for yourself as an individual. Continue favorite activities, such as gardening, taking classes of various kinds, sewing, painting, or woodworking. The sense of satisfaction you feel from taking part in these activities and nourishing yourself will make it possible for you to deal better with upsetting or less satisfying aspects of your life. If there's nothing coming in to fill your internal reservoir, you can feel empty—and then you will have nothing to give to those around you!
6. Use the rest of your time together to strengthen your couple relationship by letting each other know your needs and working out ways to satisfy them. It will be tricky when you each have different feelings about a similar person, thing, or activity. Then you will need to be creative and seek compromise.

Perhaps one of you needs time alone each day to relax and read, listen to music or simply "putter around," while the other likes to have emotional or conversational contact whenever the two of you are together. Obviously both can't happen. If, however, you each seriously consider and respect the needs of the other, it is likely that you will find a satisfactory, though not perfect, arrangement. Perhaps a certain time can be set aside for the one who needs some "alone" time, while the other person knows when to count on having the "together" time that is important to that person.

7. Make new friends if one or both of you are uncomfortable with friends from the past. Sometimes "old friends" find it difficult to accept a new partnership, and may act in ways to exclude and thus hurt the new person. This can make for difficulty between the two of you. Making new friends together, on the other hand, can help you feel closer as a couple.

The above suggestions are even more important when you have children from a previous marriage with you. Not only are you trying to form a strong couple relationship, but you are also living under the same roof with children whom you may not know well or know only from time-limited contacts during which all have been on their best behavior. Living with children means that the pulls within the household and the pulls from outside are stronger and it is more difficult to resist spending all of your precious together time dealing with guilt and anger and simple (or not so simple) logistic arrangements concerning how Becky will get to dancing class and Sue will get home from scouts.

Under these conditions it becomes even more important for you to *plan* (or it will probably never happen) time for things you each enjoy and for the two of you to be alone and do things you both like, such as taking a walk together, going out to dinner, going to the movies, visiting an art gallery or going to the local car races.

One of the feelings that often stand in the way of a couple's planning and actually doing things with each other is guilt at leaving the children. It may feel to a remarried parent as though he or she is betraying the relationship with the children to form this new important adult relationship. However, without a good couple relationship, you may not stay together and then the children, as well as you, will go through another traumatic time of loss and change. In addition, although they may fuss about not always being included, your children need to see a couple enjoying each other and doing things together as a model they can copy when they grow up. How terrible to grow up thinking that all that couples do is work, fight, scold, look serious or cry!

Stepparent-stepchild relationships

Edie was married for the first time to Anthony, who won custody of his young son Bobby soon after they were married. Anthony and Edie found themselves quarreling a lot about the lack of relationship between Edie and her stepson. Edie stated it this way: "I have a very strong husband and he expects a lot of me. Before we were married he said, 'If you take me, you take my son too,' and he expects me to really love his son. I feel guilty about having Bobby. Bobby's mother lost her home and then we took her child away from her. At times I want Bobby to really love his mother, and at other times I don't.

"Sometimes I don't know where my feelings for my husband leave off and my feelings for Bobby begin. Am I doing this or that for Bobby because it's what I want to do for him, or am I doing it because it will please Anthony?

"Bobby is a darling boy and nice to me, and that makes me feel all the more guilty that I don't love him. I think Bobby may feel the same pressure too—that he *should* love me. My husband doesn't understand how I can feel the way I do."

Edie's feelings got so strong that they began to interfere with her work as well as with her leisure time. She sought professional counseling and soon the situation began to change. Edie felt that she had to keep all her feelings of annoyance to herself in regards to Bobby since she didn't love him. She also felt that because of her lack of caring she should leave all decisions about Bobby up to her husband and his ex-wife. As a result, Anthony and his ex-wife spent considerable time on

---

Caring relationships take time to evolve. The expectation of "instant love" between stepparents and stepchildren can lead to many disappointments and difficulties. If the stepfamily relationships are allowed to develop as seems comfortable to the individuals involved, then caring between step-relatives has the opportunity to develop.

the telephone or over coffee talking about Bobby, and Edie felt left out, helpless, and depressed.

The counselor helped Edie understand that it would take time for her to form a close relationship with Bobby, but that she needed to have input into the plans that were made concerning Bobby as they affected her household. Slowly Edie began to express her needs within the household and she took part in planning with Anthony what was going to take place with Bobby. When would the three of them go away for a vacation? How long could Bobby stay out playing with his friends after supper? What weekends was Bobby going to be with his mother?

As she began to consider herself a part of this household, Edie's sense of her own worth grew stronger and stronger and she became able to tell Bobby to stop messing up the kitchen and not to take the sofa pillows outside.

Most of Edie's resentment at Bobby melted away as she was able to let him know what she needed of him, and as a result their relationship slowly began to improve. Edie started reading bedtime stories to Bobby, and he looked forward to these special times with his stepmother.

Anthony no longer needed to have contact with his ex-wife that excluded Edie, and he was also able to relax and stand back as Edie and Bobby's relationship developed. After a few months the household was running as smoothly as households can be expected to run, and Edie was able to say, "I really like Bobby so much now, and I'm having a lot of fun with him. Anthony and I are doing a lot of things together now also, and I don't feel left out and unappreciated anymore."

No matter how long the children are with you—all the time, three days a week, every other weekend or three weeks in the summer—new relationships are continually developing between stepparents and stepchildren. Of course, the better these relationships, the happier everyone will be.

One of the hardest things to do, and yet the most important thing of all, is to take it easy and let these new relationships grow slowly. If you are a parent who has remarried, you probably are very anxious to have your children and your new spouse like each other. In fact, you may not have thought about how very much you want them to really love each other. Very often stepparents say, "I'm expected to love my stepchildren because I love their parent, but I don't feel that way. This makes me feel very guilty and I try so hard, but we just don't get along." Whenever you try very hard to *feel* a certain way about someone, it usually doesn't work. You just feel the way you feel, and what happens between you and your stepchildren will help determine how your feeling relationship develops.

Stepmothers and stepdaughters seem to have a particularly difficult time developing a positive relationship. A daughter may have spent time cooking for and taking care of her father when she was with him before he remarried. With the remarriage, that particular type of father-daughter relationship is changed and the daughter feels "unemployed" and less important to her father and as if she has lost him to her stepmother.

A 15-year-old girl put it this way: "I put my stepmother and my stepfather in different categories. It's harder relating to my stepmother because I think girls need the closeness of their mother. Also I feel jealous of my stepmother because now I don't feel so worthwhile because there is a stepmother there to take over the role I'd had with my father before he remarried."

Boys, on the other hand, identify with their fathers and, especially when their father has moved out, they feel sorry for him and want to visit with him. Teenage boys are usually angry with their mothers and often seek to live with their fathers after a remarriage. If the boy has lost a special role as "man of the house" when his mother remarries, he

Being a stepparent is an unclear and at times difficult task. The wicked stepmother myth contributes to the discomfort of many women, and cultural, structural and personal factors affect the stepparent role. Spouses can be very helpful to one another if they are able to be supportive with the working out of new family patterns. Stepparenting is usually more successful if stepparents carve out a role for themselves that is different from and does not compete with the biological parents.

may become very resentful of this new adult who is coming in and taking his place.

In one single-parent household, 16-year-old Laura had been doing all the cooking for her father, and then in walked her new stepmother to rearrange the kitchen and make it hers. In another household, 12-year-old Bruce had taken pride in being allowed to mow the front lawn, but his duty was taken over by his stepfather when his mother remarried. Bruce felt displaced.

While there is still much to be learned about what happens between stepparents and stepchildren and how to deal effectively with them, here are guidelines that seem to be helpful:

- Do not come on like a ball of fire. This can cause your stepchildren to feel somewhat overwhelmed.
- Hold back and let your stepchildren approach you. Be available, but let them approach at their own pace.
- Acknowledge that the relationship between you and your stepchildren is just forming. Children often say, "She can't really love me because she really doesn't know me," or "How can he really like me—I've only known him a couple of months and even at school it takes longer than that for me to make friends." So if you say that you love them right off the bat, your stepchildren usually won't believe you and may discredit other things you say.
- Remember that your stepchildren will be different from children raised by you. They have grown up in a different environment. If you try to "make them over" it will get in the way of developing a good relationship with them. Naturally there need to be agreed upon household rules so that the members can live cooperatively together, but working out rules is different from working out a new pattern of being a person and asking someone to squeeze into this new shape. Individuals do change as they grow and mature, but the changes come from within and are patterned on many experiences throughout life. Often stepchildren absorb many of the special patterns you may be bringing into their lives, but only later on do they decide to act differently from before. This happens in all types of families. Many young adults, who now comb their hair, brush their teeth, polish their shoes and work at satisfying jobs, at 12 or 15 would "laze around all day long," with torn clothes and stringy unkempt hair!

- Each child, of course, is an individual with his or her own temperament, strengths and weaknesses. Acceptance of that self is of prime importance. Said one 14-year-old boy: "I think 75 percent of parents and stepparents have *their* ideas of how the children ought to be, rather than taking them as they are and guiding them."
- Find out what things your stepchildren like and, if possible, see that they are available. Having a basketball hoop put on the garage or finding "Dad's Old Fashioned Root Beer" in the refrigerator can give a stepchild the sense of being counted and appreciated.
- Do things with stepchildren alone without their parent being with you, especially activities the children enjoy—for example, going out for a soft drink on a hot day, helping with a project your stepchild is doing for a science fair, going fishing or picking out school clothes.
- If you are a remarried parent who sees your own children less than you'd like and feel guilty that you have caused upset for them, do your best not to let these feelings of guilt stop you from enjoying your stepchildren. You are not taking anything away from your own children by forming a good relationship with your stepchildren. There are no limits to love—there is plenty for everyone.
- You will feel differently about your stepchildren than you do about your own children. And those children who have not grown up with you will feel differently about you than they feel about their biological parents. Knowing each other and sharing yourselves and your time can produce a very special relationship, but only if you can accept that the feelings are different in the beginning and cannot be forced to bloom.
- If you are a remarried parent, you will be able to help the relation-

Forming new relationships within the stepfamily can be important, particularly when the children are young. Activities involving different subgroups can help such relationships grow. For example, stepfather and stepchildren might do some project together, or stepmother and a stepchild might go shopping together.

ship between your child and his or her stepparent if you accept that your reactions to your child and your spouse's reactions to your "darling little six-year-old" *are* different. Stand back, but support your spouse as he or she begins to relate to your children. If you feel guilty about having caused your children pain, you may find it very difficult not to try to push your spouse and your children to make this the relationship you have dreamed about. Do your best to avoid this—feeling *forced* to relate in certain ways usually brings just the opposite reaction and then you will be disappointed and unhappy, and so will your spouse and your children.

- You are different from any other adult in your stepchildren's lives. You have your own special qualities and talents to give. Perhaps you are fun-loving and playful or like hiking and other outdoor activities. Seeing these qualities in an adult may be a unique experience for your stepchildren. These dimensions can add a richness to their lives that they would otherwise have missed. Use your unique talents rather than involving yourself in areas of similarity where you and your stepchildren's biological parent may start to compete with one another. Anne Simon, in her book, *Stepchildren in the Family*, put it clearly when she said,

  A sensitive stepparent will skirt areas staked out by the child's own parent if he listens with the hearing aid of conscious respect for the other relationship. To him, "Dad says he will teach me to sail" is not a signal for stepfather to dash out to the closest shipyard, but a directive to stay in dry dock.

- Sometimes stepparent-stepchild relationships remain strained because there are so many mixed emotions floating around. Often, when the stepchildren become adults, they form new and independent relationships with stepparents. Many adult stepchildren have said that, although they resented and fought their stepparents from morning until night, they now have warm and very good relationships with them. Leave the door open, and later on you may suddenly receive a Mother's Day card, a Father's Day greeting, a birthday present from a stepchild . . . or warm telephone calls or letters, and a pleasant visit together. Knowing the effort that has gone into developing these relationships makes such incidents warm and especially rewarding.

Parent-child relationships

With a remarriage, there is a shift in the parent-child relationships that have been built up during the single-parent household phase. During the time when you lived with your children or had your children with you from time to time, depending on custody and visitation arrangements, you formed a special unit of some sort. If you drew very close together, you may be finding it hard to let another person or persons join your tight little group. And even though you may want to include your new partner and stepchildren (if you have any), your own children may be resisting and dragging their heels all the way. They don't want to have another person telling them what to do, or they think you've completely changed since you got married and they feel they've lost you. One young man outlined it this way as he spoke of the feelings he'd had as a young boy when his father remarried:

> My perception of what happened was that you, Dad, really went away, I mean completely. Your personality as I knew it was gone, and the man I knew as my father was completely gone. You and everything I knew of you were completely submerged into your relationship with Christy. No longer did I feel as though I had a father at all because I didn't know you anymore.

There usually needs to be a shift in your relationships with your children after you are remarried, for you now have a new adult relationship which will remain a primary relationship for you, hopefully, long after your children have grown and left home and formed primary adult relationships of their own. There are some ways, however, in which you can make the transition easier and the sense of loss less acute for your children, at the same time as you are working out your new stepfamily relationships:

- Reduce your children's feelings of loss as they share you with your new partner, and perhaps with other children, by continuing to have some times alone with them, the length of time depending on what will work out for other members of your household. Perhaps you and your son can go to a ballgame while your wife is shopping with her children; or you can go swimming with your daughter, while the other stepfamily members are on the shore hunting for shells; or you can go to the store for ice cream with your son, while your husband is busy working in his shop. The times together don't need to be long in minutes or hours. Your children have been used to having you to themselves and now a little time concentrating just on them is very important.

It is likely that your children will want as much exclusive time as you can give them—and more. They may even see your special times with them as paving the way for a return to your single-parent status or even a reconciliation with your former spouse. So do not be dismayed if you need to set limits on the amount of time you will be alone with them. Even though they complain, you can let them know you understand that they would like continued undivided attention, but that it is not possible. And if they continue to complain and you make it clear that continued complaints will not change the situation, most likely they will stop asking for more and enjoy the fun things you do together. Naturally, as the family is together longer, new patterns of doing things will evolve.

- Because you have had an exclusive relationship with your children, you may have mixed feelings about their forming relationships with your new spouse. On the one hand, you want them to like each other and get along well together, but on the other hand, you may feel a sense of loss yourself as your children make a spot in their lives for a stepparent. If you find these two different feelings competing inside yourself, you may want to share them with your spouse so he or she understands that you want your children and your spouse to form a new relationship and yet are sometimes tempted to stand in the way of their fragile friendship. Or perhaps when you realize the mixture of feelings you do have, you can let go of wanting to keep people apart from each other, since this lessens the amount of stepfamily enjoyment you can all have.

Preserving original relationships is also important and can help children experience less loss at sharing a parent. So at times it is helpful for a parent and biological children to have some time together, in addition to stepfamily activities.

• If you are a remarried parent seeing your children much less than you would like, you may feel guilty and be very tempted to over-compensate on weekends by crowding in a football game, a movie, the zoo, and three banana splits. This can be upsetting to your stepchildren since they feel that you don't like them very much, planning all this activity only when your children are in the household. Your spouse may also be upset, feel unappreciated and think that what your children want to do is all that matters to you. Your children, as well as the rest of your stepfamily, may feel more relaxed and contented if you accept the fact that being together is the important element. While it's fun to do some special activities, it's also nice to hang around the house and play games, watch TV or work on special projects. And, despite their cries of indignation, you and your spouse may even leave all the children when you want to do something important to the two of you.

Step-sibling relationships

Recently we met a stepfamily in which each adult had two children from a previous marriage. Although the remarriage was in its early stages and many situations were still being worked out, the household was running fairly smoothly. It turned out that the two oldest children, each one having been the oldest in the single-parent households, had become good friends, while the two younger children did many things together and were developing similar interests in baseball and hockey. The fact that these pairs of step-siblings were enjoying each other appeared to be hastening the integration process in this stepfamily. The adults were being careful to see that family rules applied to all four equally, and the children had each found a new and interesting step-sibling to pal around with.

Often step-siblings get along well when they do not have to deal with jealousies that arise because they feel "unequal treatment" in the household. As one girl put it, "I could really like my stepsister because I was free to do it. No one said I *had* to like her." Making it easy for the step-siblings in your household to do things together that they might enjoy is a way you can help the formation of these new relationships.

Again, a word of caution: If you try to promote good relationships between the children, there can be a feeling of pressure, and then things generally go downhill rather than uphill.

It can be particularly difficult for parents joining two families if there are two children of the same sex and age. If this is your situation, remember that Ted and Carl may be the same age, or Cindy and Virginia may both be 15, but that does not mean that the two children will be similar in other respects. Ted and Carl, growing up in different families, will probably be very, very different. Ted may be an active, noisy, athletic little boy with a whole host of friends, while Carl is quiet, likes to read and listen to his stereo, and has one or two close friends. Cindy and Virginia are both young women, but Cindy may be maturing physically much less quickly than Virginia, so that Cindy still plays with younger children and cares little about her looks, while Virginia spends two hours every morning getting ready for school and alternates between elation and despair depending on the current status of her social life.

If you try to make one of the pair be more like the other, then one becomes the "model" and the other child feels rejected and angry, not only at parent and stepparent, but also at the other young person. Good relationships between the step-siblings will not grow under these conditions. Each child is an individual with his or her own particular likes and dislikes, as well as strengths and weaknesses. Supporting individual likes and strengths can help each child feel accepted and remove many seeds of jealousy that otherwise could grow and produce endless fighting among the step-siblings.

If you think about it for a minute, you can undoubtedly think of many families of all types in which the children in the family are competitive with each other, or jealous and bitter towards one another. Usually these fights diminish as children grow older and as adults they may again become the best of friends. Step-siblings, as well as siblings, go through stormy times together. The major help that parents and stepparents can be is in accepting the differentness of the new youngsters dropped into their nest and allowing them to form their own relationships within the family according to how they feel most comfortable.

Unexpected instant children

Sometimes when remarried parents and stepparents talk about some stress they may be having in their family, the response they receive is an unsupportive, "Well, you knew what you were getting into." This is not a response generally given to parents married for the first time who talk about difficulties they may be having in their biological family. The difference may be that when you have children of your own there is continual speculation about what the sex will be, then whom they look like, and what they will be like as they grow up. Because the children are "already there" in stepfamilies, it may be that people not experiencing stepfamily life feel that everything is "there" to be evaluated. This, of course, is very far from the truth.

When you take a job, you may know all the members in the office and what your job description is, but it is only after you have been working there for a while that you begin to deal with the nuances of the interpersonal relationships and the shifts within the office that inevitably take place. If you don't like what is going on, you can find a new job. But if you find things you don't like in your stepfamily, it is not something to be solved by moving on to a new and possibly more satisfying position.

Many adults know which children will be with them in their new marriage, although they cannot forsee the eventual interactions. However, a large number of adults remarry expecting never to have any contact, or only minimal contact, with children from a previous marriage who are living with their other biological parent—and then out of the blue they have an unexpected, instant family. "My stepchildren's mother suddenly died when we were married only three months —and all at once we had three teenagers living with us," said one stepmother. "We went to the door and there were my husband's two children, suitcases in hand, dropped off by their mother as a Thanksgiving Day present to live with us," said another stepmother. "Two weeks before our child was born, my husband's ex-wife became ill and his three children moved in with us," reported another woman.

The shock and sudden disruption of plans, as well as the reorganization required, are difficult to imagine. If this has happened to you, you have probably felt immediate panic and disbelief, followed by a sense of helplessness and being in a stuck place. Children are not kittens that can be returned to the animal shelter nor are these neighbor children to be watched for a few hours and then returned to their homes down the block; they are bewildered, rejected children with no other home to go to. And besides that, one of you brought them into the world and perhaps loved and cared for them for a number of years before the pain of losing contact with them.

It is usually the man's children who arrive suddenly and often unannounced. In many stepfamilies, the couple has already decided that they do not want to have any children, and for these "childless" couples to suddenly be faced with one, two or sometimes more children as permanent members of the household is profoundly disturbing. The flood of feelings is overwhelming—fear, guilt, sadness, anger, and a sense of confusion as physical and emotional space is hurriedly found for the children.

Stepfamilies try hard to adjust to the unexpected additions to their family. After the initial shock, plans are worked out, bedrooms shared, schools found, and regrouping and reorganization take place. The "new" children may continue to feel very insecure and to wonder if they really are wanted. In fact, they may test in various ways to find out. Tina, a ten-year-old girl left on her father and stepmother's doorstep, said reluctantly, after a number of months in her new household, that she wanted to return to live with her mother. Her father and stepmother guessed, apparently correctly, that she really needed to know if she was wanted in their home, and so they answered by saying, "We don't want you to go to live with your mother. We want you to live here with us. If you still want to live with her when you're 14, we'll talk about it then." "Okay," said Tina as she ran off happily to play.

If you are in a stepfamily in which you have had the experience of unexpected instant children and have not been able to work satisfactory solutions for the family, we strongly suggest that you find a counselor skilled in working with individuals in stepfamilies. Talking with a skilled person not involved personally with your family can help you make necessary decisions.

When a stepfamily is created, there are usually many prior bonds and alliances, in particular, the parent-child relationships. We have suggested a number of ways to slowly shift the alliances so that all members of your stepfamily will feel included and related to each other. Above all, you and your spouse need to be sure you nourish your own relationship so that you have an adult unit that can guide the family on its way. As adults you do have the power to preserve the family unit. Sensing that you support and care for each other, the children will be more comfortable knowing that there is a solid foundation to your family unit. There may be many complicated situations to work out, but keeping the communication channels open between you and your spouse and between the adults and the children gives you a good basic start for working out many satisfactory solutions to the challenges that arise.

6 | Dealing With Former Spouses

One of the most difficult areas for many, many stepfamilies is dealing with the fact that the children have another biological parent elsewhere, either in reality or in memory—a former spouse of at least one of the adults. This is a "hot" area because of the strength of the feelings seething under the surface or erupting with sudden and explosive force from time to time.

Guilt, anger and pain—leftovers from the past

Anger and guilt can tie two people together as tightly as love. You may not have wanted the divorce and you may still be reeling from the rejection and pain that it caused you. Even though you have remarried, you may not have let yourself feel and then forget the hurt from the past; instead, you may still be fighting and trying to get back at your ex-spouse. Fighting with and blaming someone else may be a way of not facing your own hurt feelings. One woman put it into words by saying, "If I'm angry I have a rigid spine, but if I'm sad and hurt I feel like a wet noodle." Most people would prefer not to see themselves as a wet noodle, so they choose to be a fighter instead.

It is a deeply painful experience to go through a divorce, particularly if it was your former spouse's idea, and there is often much sadness and loneliness and tears. If you haven't let yourself really mourn the losses, as well as be angry at the hurt and pain, then you may still be fighting with your ex-spouse over alimony, child support, visitation rights or the way he or she is treating the children. It is almost impossible to let go of the anger until you have accepted the disappointment that your original dreams didn't work out as you'd planned. As one minister said, "The healing of memories takes time." Letting go of the hurt, as well as the anger, makes it possible for you to forgive an ex-spouse— and that can make you feel freer of the past and ready to enjoy your present. A more relaxed attitude on your part can also create more contentment for all the others in your household.

Guilt may be an even stronger feeling for you than anger, especially if you were the one who wanted the divorce. You may continue to be angry and quarrel with your former spouse partly because you feel guilty at having caused him or her pain, but also because you have upset your children. You may find yourself unable to separate from the past. Because of this, people in your new household unit may feel that you are not truly committed to your stepfamily unit. Your present spouse may feel unappreciated and insecure; your children may continue to act in all sorts of annoying ways because they hope they can somehow reverse things and bring about the "good old days" as they remember them; and your stepchildren may feel rejected by you if you hold yourself back from relating to them because your guilt creates a barrier. You may even feel guilty that you can provide material and emotional gifts to your stepchildren that you are unable to give to your biological children.

Your guilt may also lead you to try to keep your ex-spouse from being angry, and often this leads to trouble in your new household. Your present spouse may get the impression that his or her feelings count much less to you than the feelings of your former spouse.

Ann and Gregory had been married for seven months. Ann had no children but Gregory had twins, Sara and Sally, from his previous marriage. Gregory had been unhappy in his first marriage and was the one who made the decision to leave, despite his wife's pleas for him to stay. Gregory was angry and hurt because of all the fighting that had taken place in his first marriage and he also felt guilty at the pain he was causing his former wife and children. Whenever his former wife asked for more money to repair her refrigerator or to buy clothes for the twins, Gregory would always say yes. After his remarriage, Gregory still found himself giving in to all the requests, even when it meant that he and Ann wouldn't have enough to take a trip they had planned or to buy a lamp Ann wanted for their home. Ann felt discounted and angry. She felt that Gregory considered the wishes of his ex-wife to be more important than her wishes. As a result, arguments between them became more frequent and resentment began to build.

Often, fear that an angry ex-spouse will not allow the child who lives in that household to come for visits adds to the anger. Because they do not want to jeopardize visitation rights, remarried parents may decide to respond to the requests and demands of the ex-spouse even though to do so causes upset in the new household.

All relationships involve more than one person. Marriage is a relationship involving two people, each of whom contributes to both the successes and failures of that relationship. No one person can be responsible for the couple relationship. To continue to carry the burden of guilt for a relationship that didn't work out ties you to the past and stands in the way of making a full commitment to your new partner. Your guilt can also prevent you from giving your children and stepchildren the love and the limit-setting they need to grow into healthy, happy adults.

When you feel good about yourself, you can handle difficult situations with much more ease than if you are feeling down on yourself. Guilt and anger lead to lowered self-esteem. Often, people in this situation feel that they have failed and cannot relate well to anyone, or that they are bad parents. These are common self-destructive reactions that follow in the wake of a divorce. If you are feeling this way, your new stepfamily responsibilities may be grinding you into the ground. Obviously, you need to gain self-confidence so that you can effectively meet your new family challenges. You need to gain an increasing sense of your strength and ability as a person so that you can handle difficult events in your life. "The weekend was awfully upsetting while it was happening," said one young stepmother, "but now I feel so pleased with the way I dealt with it, and that makes me feel good about myself."

The fact that you have been divorced does not mean that you are a failure or unlovable. Very nice people don't always fit together. Intimacy is difficult to achieve, and both you and your former spouse may have had trouble developing a close relationship. New insights, experiences and personal growth may have changed this for you.

There are several ways in which stepparents and remarried parents can gain needed self-confidence:

- Reading books dealing with divorce and remarriage families. (A list is given in Appendix B.)

- Talking to friends or acquaintances who have been divorced and remarried.

- Joining an organization whose purpose is to provide educational and/or supportive services for stepfamilies. For example:

  1. Stepfamily Association of America, Inc.
     215 Centennial Mall S., Suite 212
     Lincoln, NE 68508

  Local chapters exist in many different states.

- Talking with a counselor or therapist who has some training and experience helping individuals in stepfamilies meet the particular challenges of this type of family.

- Attending workshops and courses specifically designed for adults in stepfamilies.

When the former spouse has died

We are often asked if stepfamily integration goes more smoothly if a former spouse is deceased rather than divorced. Not having to deal with an ex-spouse in person does appear to relieve some of the tensions between the new couple. Remarriages which occur following the death of a spouse tend to have a better statistical chance of lasting than those where an ex-spouse is still alive. However, the children in stepfamilies formed after the death of one of their parents often have to deal with a greater sense of loss and more intense loyalty conflicts. To them it may appear as though the new couple relationship ends the former marriage—that their surviving parent really didn't care about the parent who has died—and as a result the children may experience more stress in this situation.

There seem to be four major challenges to be faced in a remarriage after the death of a spouse:

1. Giving yourself and your children
enough time to mourn the loss
of the person who has died

Recognize that you may have a tendency to plunge into new relationships to ease the pain and loneliness long before your children are ready to accept new adults in their lives. To them the remarriage may seem "too quick" and so they may fight the new relationship.

You may find yourself clinging to ways "my wife used to do it" or "my husband would have said it" because you have tried to go on with your life before saying your final good-byes. If this is true, you may find yourself talking about your former spouse a great deal, clinging to material possessions and ways of doing things from the past, which can be sources of irritation to your new family, or being unable to let your children (particularly the youngest or "last" one) grow up and leave home to be on their own. If you or your children are aware of the difficulties in this area, you may want to talk to a religious counselor or join a group or class designed to help you experience your feelings of loss and sadness or other feelings around the death of your former spouse.

Once you have completed your mourning, you will no longer be struggling with feelings from the past and your new family unit will be able to grow closer and work out its own new ways of doing things.

2. Making the dead person into a saint

When there is a live ex-spouse in the picture, it is usually easy to remember his or her human frailties. In fact, many ex-spouses have practically sprouted horns according to their former mates! In contrast, when a partner has died, as time passes it is very easy to forget annoyances or even gross incompatibilities. The memories which remain tend to be positive. As a result, the person who has died often becomes idealized—and it is virtually impossible for a new spouse to compete with a saint!

If you remember that former spouses who are no longer alive were human, just like you and your present spouse, then your new partner will be able to feel more secure in your new relationship and the children will have less opportunity to compare their new stepparent with the image of an unrealistic superhuman-being.

3. Attempting to "replace" the spouse who has died

Particularly when you have had a good relationship with your former spouse who has died, it is a temptation to try to "replace" this person with someone you perceive as being similar in many ways. There certainly may be many similarities because you have learned what kind of a person you would like to be married to, but if you think of him or her as a "replacement," your new spouse will not feel loved and appreciated for himself or herself and your relationship can suffer. No two people are the same, and having a good relationship with a new person has nothing to do with your former relationships. If you work at it, you may have the experience of two good marriages. Your children also need to know that you feel that each partnership was special, so that they can also enjoy your present family unit, without needing to compare it to the past. Having a warm and satisfying family experience in the present does not detract from what has gone before.

4. Money and inheritance

Many older people remarry after the death of a spouse, creating 25-year-old, 35-year-old, or 45-year-old "stepchildren." Family rearrangements of any kind at any age can be unsettling, and older "stepchildren" and the new older couple are usually startled to find that they are dealing with feelings very similar to those experienced by younger children and adults. There is non-acceptance of the new "stepparent," as well as fear, loss and pain at all the changes.

There is also another fear that occurs more strongly when older couples remarry, and that concerns money and inheritance. "What is going to happen to my mother's jewelry?" "My stepmother gave away some of the books that were my mother's without even asking me if I wanted them." "I wonder if Donald and mother are writing new wills and if we will be included?" "What is going to happen to the house I grew up in for 25 years?"

If you are older and have remarried or plan to remarry, you can avoid much hurt and anxiety if you:

- Talk to your older children and their families about your plans.
- Inform your children about the contents of your will, discussing your wishes with them and getting their reaction or suggestions if you are comfortable doing so.
- Let them have "first choice" of any items, no matter how unimportant they may seem to you, before you dispose of them. As one older stepson said, "I would have been willing to *buy* my father's old telescope, but it was given away before I even had a chance."
- Include children and grandchildren in special family times so that they have the opportunity to get used to all the changes. Peter found it spoiled his Thanksgiving to see another man in his

father's chair at the end of the table, carving the turkey as his father had done for so many years. Peter and his mother realized without actually talking about it that the pattern for Thanksgiving needed to be changed. The next year the celebration was held at Peter's home, and he sat at the head of the table and carved the turkey. As life moves on, rituals can be changed without destroying the happy memories of the past.

- If possible, give children a few special items that belonged to their parent who has died, so that they feel that you are willing to accept and honor their past history and memories.
- Seek the advice of an attorney before you marry to help you divide your property in a way that is fair and comfortable for you both for the present and for the future, considering that you have grown children. For example, Anita and Charles each had owned a home and had savings accounts for many years. Their spouses died, and before they remarried they had an attorney draw up an agreement whereby Anita's children would eventually share in the assets that were hers at the time of the remarriage. Similar arrangements were made for Charles' children.

When one parent remarries

Sharing children is one of the most difficult and disturbing things you may ever be called upon to do. This is especially true when one parent has not remarried. Custody and visitation arrangements can play a part in the feelings of loss of control or helplessness which each adult feels, and children many times get caught in the middle between angry ex-spouses.

When one parent remarries and the other one does not, many emotionally insecure and painful questions arise for the unmarried parent:

- "Now will he want custody of Judy?"
- "Will Carol like her new stepparent better than she likes me?"
- "There's a real home there now, and I can't offer Johnnie a home because there's only me here."

Very often unmarried parents feel scared that their children will want to live with their remarried parent instead of where they have been living. This fear of more loss and more loneliness on the part of the unmarried parent can lead to many bitter disagreements over where the children are staying, for how long and how they are being treated when they are in the other household. If you are the remarried parent, it can help everyone if you remember that many self-doubts and insecurities are being stirred up inside your children and your ex-spouse.

It takes a lot of inner security as a parent to feel that your single-parent household can be as good for children as the household with two adults (and perhaps with other children as well). If you are the unmarried parent, remember that you are really still just as important to your children as you have ever been, and they continue to need the particular things you have to offer them as much as they ever did. They may worry that you are lonely and realize that their other parent is no longer lonely, so it is important to do your best not to burden them with the feeling that they need to look after you. They will be much happier if they do not have to feel that they are responsible for your happiness, and you will have a better relationship with them. They will grow to be independent adults more easily if they do not feel the need to "take care" of you.

If you are the first to remarry, shift living arrangements, visiting arrangements or custody agreements as gradually as possible so that there is time for everyone involved to know what is going on and adjust to the changes. When changes are made, if they can be mutually agreed upon by the adults it will reduce the loyalty conflicts of the children and both households will function more smoothly.

Using children as messengers between households

Because of the deep and troublesome emotions mentioned earlier in this chapter, many ex-spouses feel like enemies. And one way to protect yourself from an enemy is by having a spy or a special messenger to bring you news about what is going on in the enemy camp. All too often your children unwittingly are pushed into the role of messenger.

When we talk with young children after a divorce and a remarriage, they cry and are confused, as if they are being tossed back and forth like a ball as their parents argue and fight.

Older children are often angry and complain bitterly about being "pumped" for information about the other parent and the stepparent or the other household. In a recent survey, adolescents in stepfamilies ranked arguments and angry "put-downs" between their divorced parents as being the most "stressful" part of their life in their stepfamily. Your children are part of you and your ex-spouse, and when you argue and are angry with your former partner it feels to your children as though you are also angry with them, since they are biologically and psychologically part of that other parent. There are ways of keeping your children out of the middle and avoiding these situations:

1. Do not involve young children in conversations regarding plans with the other biological parent. Work the arrangements out between the adults, in person, by telephone, by letter, or whatever way produces less tension and therefore better results. A young child should not be asked to make decisions about visitation arrangements, for example. The parent who has custody is responsible for seeing that the other parent has a fair opportunity to be with the children. Studies have shown that children who have contact with both parents on a regular basis in divorce situations

---

Courteous relationships between ex-spouses are important, although they are very difficult for many adults to maintain. If such a relationship can be worked out, it is especially helpful to the children. In such instances the children do not get caught in the middle between two hostile parents, there is less need for the children to take sides, and the children are better able to accept and utilize the positive elements in their living arrangements.

Direct contact between the adults can be helpful since it does not place the children in the sometimes powerful position of being message carriers between their biological parents. Although it may be strained, many ex-spouses are able to relate in regards to their children if the focus is kept on their mutual concern for the welfare of the children.

are able to adjust better than when the contact is nonexistent and they continue to relate to both parents in a positive manner. Sometimes young children sense the unhappiness of the parent with whom they stay most of the time, and are reluctant to leave. So they may say, "I don't like to go to Daddy's house—it's no fun." However, if you simply treat the visits as a matter of course, with as few changes as possible in the schedule, this lifts the pressure and says to the children, "It's okay to go."

2. If all the adults—parents and stepparents—can talk together about arrangements, so much the better. If not, have the adults who can relate together the most easily communicate with each other. Often ex-spouses cannot have a successful contact, but the stepparent in one household and the biological parent in the other household can work out the plans more comfortably. In other situations the two stepparents can work out the arrangement for the two households. Use whatever mode of communication works and leaves your children out of the middle.

3. Encourage older children to have input about arrangements affecting them before making the contact with the other household to work out the necessary details.

4. If there are tension and anger between you and your ex-spouse, talk to him or her when your children are not around. In this way you will avoid upsetting your children.

5. Expect only general conversation about their other household from your children. If you ask pointed questions, they may feel intruded upon or expected to be a spy or messenger.

6. Sometimes children love to talk about all the terrible or wonderful happenings in their other household. When they are doing this, you may find that they are placing themselves in a very powerful position by stirring up feelings in all the adults. ("Mushing things around and stirring up the pot," to quote one remarried parent.) Having this kind of power does not work out well for anyone, and you can put an end to "playing one household off against the other" by discouraging and not responding to this behavior by your children and by talking directly with the adult or adults in the other household.

7. If the adults simply cannot talk, find a counselor to act as a facilitator (and referee, if necessary!) for the adults, so that the children are not acting as messengers or pawns and are not caught in the middle. Children can usually adjust well to the stresses of di-

vorce and remarriage as long as the level of tension and animosity between their parents is kept low.

The need for household boundaries

A remarried father with custody of his three children came to see us one day asking the question, "Do I have to check with my ex-wife before I do anything with the children like going to the zoo, or taking them on a trip to see my parents for the weekend?" Another time a stepmother asked in tears, "What's wrong with me? I feel so jealous when my husband's ex-wife calls up and asks him to come and mow her lawn and fix her washing machine and off he goes and I don't see him for the whole afternoon." And in another stepfamily the remarried mother included her ex-husband in their special celebrations and her new husband said, "I suppose that's a good way to do it, but I feel uncomfortable—like I'm on the outside looking in."

It seems to us that all these questions and feelings arise from difficulty in knowing what the rules are in a remarried family. What are the boundaries around the family? Whom should be included when? What rights do second wives or second husbands have? And these questions arise because there have been no generally accepted guidelines and ways of doing things that have grown up over the years and are simply part of the way stepfamilies do things. Biological families differ greatly in many ways, but generally procedures have been established by society—parents and children in a family are not expected to consult anyone else before carrying out their day-to-day plans, husbands and wives expect to have the right to give input into the way the family will operate, and husbands do not automatically spend time taking care of other people's homes except under special circumstances understood and agreed upon by both adults.

Because the structure of stepfamilies is different and there is a biological parent of the children in another household, a new dimension exists, and the boundary around the family becomes fuzzy. However, if the boundary around your stepfamily household is not clearly defined, you may experience a sense of confusion or anxiety.

The children are members of two households and must deal with two separate household boundaries, which we diagrammed earlier like this:

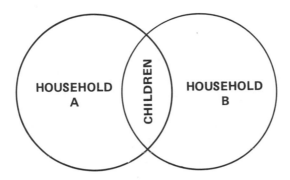

Although stepfamily boundaries need to be less distinct than when only one household exists, so that children can move back and forth between two households, if you do not have clear household boundaries you may feel very insecure and so may the children. An adolescent or young adult needs to feel like a separate individual with his or her own personal boundary before he or she is able to relate comfortably with other family members. In the same way, a stepfamily household needs to experience its own separateness and boundaries before there can be a comfortable relationship between parents and stepparents in the children's two households.

Some stepfamilies have developed patterns which work for them (but not necessarily for everyone) in which both sets of parents may spend special times together with their shared children. The children in one stepfamily prepared a special Father's Day celebration which was attended by their mother and stepfather with whom they lived, and also by their father who lived in another town. In another case, a stepfamily household consisting of Martha and Jim, her child and one of his two children invited Jim's ex-wife and his other child to stay with them at the time of Jim's son's graduation from high school. We believe that the blending of two households in ways illustrated by these examples is comfortable or at least relatively comfortable for everyone only after each household has established its own boundaries and members are aware at some level that the boundaries do exist and that there is a true separation from the past emotional ties of the adults. But for many stepfamilies, getting together as just outlined is never an alternative.

If you feel, as many stepparents do, that there are "ghosts" living in your house, then you and your partner have not yet created clear boundaries around your household. Often a spouse expresses the feeling by saying that there are three adults in the household—"me, my husband, and his ex-wife" or "me, my wife, and her ex." There are a number of common reasons why this may happen:

- You have not really gone through the sadness of saying good-bye to your past relationship and dreams, and so you keep hanging on in little ways to your former spouse.
- Your ex-spouse has not yet separated psychologically and said good-bye to you, and so keeps coming over, telephoning, wanting to know all about the children, etc.
- If you asked for the divorce, you keep wanting your ex-spouse to say that he or she understands why you needed to leave and that you are a really good person.
- If you did not wish the divorce, you keep wanting your ex-spouse to say that you are a really special person and it was his or her own problems that precipitated the divorce.
- You fear your ex-spouse will not let you see your children if you do not keep in close contact and do whatever he or she wishes.

Until stepfamily boundaries have been established that are comfortable for the individuals in your household, you may continue to wonder and worry and feel uncomfortable about many situations involving ex-spouses. Here are some guidelines that you may find helpful:

1. If you have not separated psychologically from your ex-spouse and it is too difficult to manage this alone, find an understanding friend or counselor to help you do it.
2. Set limits on telephone conversations, letters, personal contacts, etc., with your former spouse if he or she has not separated from you psychologically.
3. Let go of the wish to receive approval and appreciation from your ex-spouse. He or she is often the last person to look to for acceptance; also, hanging on to wanting approval from your former

partner may be stopping you from hearing and enjoying the love and appreciation you *are* receiving from your spouse, your family and others.

4. Make decisions involving your own household with the members of your particular stepfamily unit.

5. Include the children's other parent in decisions involving them, for example, vacation arrangements, piano lessons that could involve the other parent as a chauffeur at certain times, Thanksgiving plans.

6. Recognize that no two households operate on the same rules. Set the ones you want for your household and let your ex-spouse set the rules for that other household. Your child may complain, "Daddy lets me stay up till 10 o'clock. I don't want to go to bed now. Why do I have to go to bed s-o-o-o early?" You can reply, for example, "Because nine o'clock is the bedtime we have in this household." In this way you are establishing the boundaries, the regulations in your household. They may be *different* from the rules in your child's other household, but families have many different ways of working out their own patterns, and children can adjust to different rules in different places.

7. Make it clear that family households do things differently. It is not a matter of there being a "right" way and a "wrong" way, though from time to time there may be a need for the adults in the children's lives to get together to discuss some extreme or upsetting situation. Unless the children are teenagers, they may not need to be included in such negotiations. One stepfather and mother, for example, were able to convince the wife's ex-husband that it was injurious to the eight-year-old son to be taken to X-rated movies. How the son dressed, or what he ate, or what time he went to bed when he was with his father, however, were items that were different in the two households, and matters that only came up for discussion and argument between the adults when they were upset and angry about something such as money. In this case the adults argued over the different house rules because they couldn't do anything about the prescribed legal monetary arrangements. To repeat: Have your own house rules, and let the children know that there may be different house rules in their other household, in their friend's household, in their grandparent's household—and that's simply the way it is!

What you decide to do about contacts with ex-spouses may change over time as you become more settled in your new marriage relationship, develop clear feelings about commitments to your present stepfamily unit and have a sense that you have a unique household with its own characteristics and its own limitations and boundaries. Whatever is eventually decided, however, will only work if all members of your household are reasonably comfortable with the decisions. It won't work to sit at a school play with your former spouse if your present spouse "grins and bears it" and then is upset. It will work, however, if you go to school conferences with your present spouse and your ex-spouse, and all the adults feel comfortable that this is the way they wish to deal with the school.

"No win" battles

Although many stepfamilies work out their relationships with ex-spouses smoothly, or relatively so, for many other stepfamilies this area of interpersonal relations is filled with emotional pain. Since remarriage is a phase in a process starting with a divorce or death of a spouse, in many families discord between the couple has started before the divorce, at times even many years prior to the divorce. At the time of the divorce, and afterwards, the bitterness and tension often continue, and in such cases remarriage tends to heighten rather than lessen already existing animosity. At other times, where divorced spouses have been able to work together amicably as parents of shared children, rejection and anger may come bubbling up at the time of the remarriage. A new adult has entered the scene and fears of more relationship losses between parents and children can heat the emotional pot to the boiling point.

A parent without custody often feels particularly vulnerable and helpless, though in many such situations the adults in *both* households feel helpless—each thinking that the other parent has all the power. From these feelings of helplessness come many court battles over custody and visitation, child support, and who is to be where when, as well as many personal battles over household rules and regulations.

Having to depend on someone you don't trust to work with you on arrangements for your children or to be civil when speaking to your new spouse—or needing to be civil yourself to your own or your part-ner's ex-spouse—may produce tensions only fully understood by those who have dealt with similar emotionally laden interactions. And in this blast furnace of emotions and the need to communicate without a basic sense of trust between the individuals, you may find yourself caught up in battle after battle in which no one wins. Indeed, it is likely that you all lose in one way or another—your children may be torn apart and react in various ways, and you may live with a knot of fear and anxiety that churns inside you and turns your stomach into raw meat. Your feelings of helplessness and anger may drive you straight up the wall and you dream of drowning everyone ten times over in one single night!

In any type of family there are many things which parents cannot control—illnesses, accidents, what kind of people your grandparents and parents were and are and many aspects in the lives of your grow-ing children. In stepfamilies control and certainty are diminished be-cause there are often powerful additional elements that influence your family unit—the children's other biological parent, added pressure from your parents (your children's grandparents), legal arrangements you dislike and the need to share children.

It takes two to have a battle. You may be used to fighting and are not especially bothered by it, but chances are that it is very upsetting to your children. If you hate the eternal power struggles you seem to be in over when your ex-spouse will return Jennie, when Carla is going to be picked up, what date the child support payment will arrive, or where the children will be this Halloween, then it is time to figure out ways of refusing to join the battle.

Of course, there are times when parents do need to protect their chil-dren from abusive parents or dangerous living situations. However, most struggles with your ex-spouse probably serve mainly as a way of getting rid of your feelings of anger at him or her rather than really solving a problem. Of course, your anger then builds up again and there is another battle which sets everyone at odds again—and so you "can't win for losing!" Court battles are costly, both emotionally and financially. The more they can be eliminated, the better for all con-cerned.

Perhaps you will find the following ideas helpful in reducing your sense of helplessness and therefore your anger, so that you can get off the battlefield and enjoy your new family relationships more and more:

Figure out what you can control in the situation. Usually people react to things they don't like by trying to get the other person to change. Sometimes the other person is willing to change, but at other times this is not the case—particularly if positive feelings and a trusting relationship are lacking. That does not mean, however, that you are helpless. It simply means that you have to figure out what *you* are going to do to make the situation work better for you.

Several common situations that arise in stepfamilies causing tension and anger are:

- The children come "dressed in rags" although you are supplying what you consider as excessive child support and had asked that they wear good clothes this weekend.
- The children are expected at a certain time and are delivered two hours later.
- You are about to leave for a weekend by yourselves at a relaxing resort when the phone rings and an ex-spouse says that he or she has something scheduled and cannot take the children for the weekend as planned.
- Your ex-spouse says negative things about you or your spouse to the children.

Some suggestions on how to make your own decisions in such a way that you control what you *can* control and avoid feelings of helplessness and anger follow:

1. If it is the first time one of the above has occurred, you may be able to talk with the children's other parent and get cooperation so that it will not happen again.
2. If it is a habitual pattern, you may blow up and no doubt spoil everyone's day! In spite of promises by the other parent, the same situation will undoubtedly arise again. This is not a good choice from your point of view, so blow up in private, hammer nails, scrub the floor, and calm down before acting.
3. You may be wishing to act as a good parent to your children and in your efforts to have them think well of their other parent you

may be protecting him or her by making many different excuses for the lateness or his or her inability to have them come for the weekend.

It will help the children if you don't blame their other parent, but by trying to "protect" the relationship between the children and their other parent you may be getting yourself in the middle between them and causing a lot of anger in yourself. Often when one parent has simply said to the children that they'll have to ask the other parent why he is late, the children do so, draw their own conclusions and form their own relationship with their other parent. You may wish it were a different kind of relationship, but that is something you can't control. And it's amazing how children are able to adjust to situations if they are clear about what these are. One mother, after protecting her ex-husband so that his children would not feel upset that he usually was late picking them up, stopped making excuses for him. This took a load off her shoulders, and much to her surprise the children didn't get upset. They knew what to expect and arranged their activities so they could be located when he did arrive, simply saying, "Dad's usually late, you know. That's just the way he is."

4. You can decide what you can control to make it work for you. If you need good clothes for your children, you can have some at your home, and then you will not go through the hassles when they come inappropriately dressed. True, it costs money, but you can probably work it out so what you spend is small compared to the relief you feel as a result of dropping out of the battle.

5. If you are unable to persuade your ex-spouse that it is very hurtful for children when bad things are said about you or your household, then one very positive thing you can do is to go on being yourself with the children. They will form their own opinions as they grow older. One mother, however, felt it was not right for her to explain to her children that her ideas were different from their father's ideas about many things. She felt caught—she had to either keep quiet entirely or blast her ex-husband. When she realized she could stand up for herself and give her viewpoint without losing control or cutting down her ex-husband, she felt free to relate more closely with her children and not worry about what their father was saying about her—they could be with her and learn to understand and accept her ways.

6. You need to be able to plan some times for yourselves, and if you

cannot count on child-care as agreed upon, then you may choose to have back-up arrangements for your children so that you are not dependent on an ex-spouse who may not come through. Staying home and feeling let down and deprived can lead to your being angry and upset with the children, who are not really responsible for your pain. The children may complain about the change of plans or may accept the change as a matter of course if alternative plans are made as a matter of course. They need caring adults who are happy and fulfilled, so they actually gain rather than lose by your paying attention to your own needs to be out from under all responsibility from time to time.

7. Keep a journal when you get upset, and write down all your feelings. This gets them out of your head and makes it easier to think about what you want to do.

8. Work together as a couple, and support one another, so that you can share ideas and help each other work out these painful situations—creating instead good times for yourselves and your family.

There are limits to what you can control in any situation in life, but within those limits there are many things that are within your own control. Figuring out what you can do that will work best for you and your particular family can remove you from many no win battles and bring more control and mastery into your household. There is no way that you can make everything work out the way that you would like it to be, and perfect solutions to problems very seldom exist. State your feelings and your ideas, negotiate as much as you can, be creative in controlling what you can control, and let the rest go. You will then not be adding to the pile of life's unhappiness, and you will instead be enjoying the good things that can take place in your life. As an old Chinese proverb states it: You cannot prevent the birds of sorrow from flying over your head, but you don't need to let them build nests in your hair.

If you really get stuck, talk with a counselor or attorney to help you sort out that you can control and/or join a mutual help group for stepfamily couples if there is one in your area. As one group member said, "Since joining this group I've saved more money in attorney's fees! And I also feel happier even though I'm not seeing my kids any more than before."

Civil relationships between ex-spouses

Everyone gains if all the parental adults involved in a child's life have a good working relationship with each other in respect to the child. Paul Bohannan, an anthropologist who has studied different family patterns, has found that in America there are a number of families where divorce and remarriage occur, the adults all become friends and an extended "kinship" group is established. This does not happen often, but when it does the children are usually very comfortable in their relationships with several adults with parental roles. In the more usual situation, where there is simply a working relationship between the adults, the children's loyalty conflicts are reduced and as a result they go between their two homes more easily and relate positively to their biological parents, as well as to their stepparents.

Studies of divorcing families have shown that the children are able to adjust to the changes and make progress with their growth and development if they continue to have access to both of their parents. A remarriage does not "replace" a biological parent; it simply adds another adult who can contribute to the children his or her own unique qualities. As before, the children continue to need their two biological parents. There is now some evidence that suggests that stepfamily integration is also easier and more likely to occur when the children continue to have a relationship with both of their biological parents. The better the relationship between the ex-spouses, the less conflicts there are for the children. If your children don't feel that they must choose between the adults in their lives, their freedom to relate to parents and to stepparents enriches their lives and helps create a positive stepfamily experience for all of you.

The idea of "co-parenting" is growing as it is recognized that, except in rare cases, children need to have this continuing relationship with both of their biological parents. *Mom's House, Dad's House* by Isolina Ricci gives guidelines for working out new ways of parenting following a divorce. We will have more to say about this in the chapter on custody and visitation.

Adults who are not able to live together as marital parents may still be able to respect the parenting skills of one another. While spouses may not have received what they needed from one another, children have their own relationship with those same adults, and since their needs are different, the children may be receiving much benefit from each parent.

You may find your ex-wife a sloppy housekeeper and unable to hold a job because of continued tardiness—but your children may find her carefree and fun-loving and full of humorous stories to make them smile. Or you may find your ex-husband grumpy and bogged down worrying about the ills of the world—but your children may find him steady and consistent and willing to help with their homework and play games with them. The two of you don't want to live together as a couple, but both of you may have parenting skills to be acknowledged and shared with your children. Limit your contacts with your ex-spouse to arrangements for the children if that is necessary, including your present spouse as well. This can avoid many heartaches. Allow yourself to experience the warmth of positive stepfamily relationships, as the children have a different and meaningful relationship with all the parental adults in their lives.

If this is a goal that seems unattainable to you at present, but one you would like to work towards, remember that time is a good healer of sad memories and ragged feelings and that many counselors and therapists are willing to help time to do its work. Even if your ex-spouse remains unwilling to work with you in this way, your own attitude and the attitude of your new partner, if positive, can contribute immeasurably to your happiness and to the happiness of your children.

7 | Grandparents of Remarriage

Pain and loss for grandparents

Parents raise their children expecting and hoping for certain special events to occur for them—satisfying jobs, friends in abundance, marriage and children. Many times it looks as though these dreams have come true, when suddenly the doorbell rings and there is their daughter Polly in tears: Polly and John are separating. They have been married for ten years, each have jobs they enjoy, and their two children Tom, eight, and Ricky, six, are loved by their parents and grandparents alike. Polly, sobbing, says that she and John have been quarreling more and more lately and have decided to get a divorce. They have gone to see a marriage counselor, but it didn't change their decision to separate—and everyone is miserable.

Like many other parents, Polly's parents have to deal with pain and loss. When parents hear about an adult child's divorce, their world is suddenly turned topsy-turvy, and they feel angry and hurt. If you are divorced, you may have been surprised by your parents' reactions when you first announced your intentions. Perhaps they tried to get you to go back to your estranged spouse, or encouraged your spouse to keep the children as an inducement for you to return to the marriage, or disowned you and would have nothing to do with you, or said that, no matter how bad the situation between the two adults, you needed to stay together for the sake of the children. In their own hurt and pain, your parents and the grandparents of your children probably lashed out angrily at you when you were feeling most vulnerable and alone. In contrast some parents may be delighted with your decision to divorce, saying, as one parent did, "We've been expecting this for years."

Even if your parents have accepted the divorce, there is frequently another psychological blow coming for them when you tell them you are planning to be remarried. Your remarriage will further change the relationship between your parents and their grandchildren, especially if your parents have cared for your children during the time you have been running a single-parent household or if you have moved back with your children into their home during a period of single parenting. If your parents have enjoyed this caretaking role and the close relationship with their grandchildren, they may feel a keen sense of loss when you remarry. The situation is further complicated when you are marrying a person with children from a previous marriage. Your parents are then being asked to adjust to your new status, a new son-in-law or daughter-in-law, possibly diminished contact with grandchildren and the presence of instant stepchildren—all at once!

Joanne had been married for 12 years and had two children, Jody and Marcia. After Joanne's divorce, Jody and Marcia spent every weekday afternoon with Joanne's parents while she worked as a teller in a nearby bank. Joanne's parents were retired and enjoyed having their grandchildren around. They helped them with their homework, took them ice skating with their friends, and spent many hours planning special times for the children.

After two years of this arrangement, Joanne developed a serious relationship with Chris. Joanne's parents, the Morgans, began to feel uneasy because Chris lived in another town and had custody of three children from his previous marriage. The Morgans did not welcome

Chris or make any attempt to get to know his children when they came with him to pick up Joanne and her children for a weekend outing. Joanne and Chris continued to see each other and after some months they announced with some misgivings that they had decided to get married.

The Morgans had difficulty controlling their sadness, and they asked to have Jody and Marcia spend more time with them. Without realizing the added difficulties this would make for her parents, Joanne urged her children to be with their grandparents more frequently, although the girls wanted more time to be with their school friends.

After the marriage, Joanne and her children moved to the town where Chris lived, and the Morgans had many feelings of loss which they tried to handle. They loved their daughter and were pleased that she seemed happy, but they felt overwhelmed by all the adjustments they were having to make all at once—lonely afternoons now that Jody and Marcia were no longer with them, less contact with Joanne who was living 30 miles away, uncomfortable visits with Chris and three strange children when they all got together on a weekend. The Morgans felt as though a tornado had struck their home and made a shambles of their lives. They were numb and unable to do more than go through their days in an unthinking, uncaring daze. There had been too many changes for them to handle all at once. But gradually they filled in the gaps in their days, began to know and care for their step-grandchildren, and once again feel comfortable with Joanne and Jody and Marcia. Then the 30 miles became a small barrier indeed to warm relationships and important times together with Joanne, Chris and all of their expanded family.

If you have not been previously married, your parents' dreams for you, like your own, may have included orange blossoms and an extended honeymoon in Tahiti . . . and here you are introducing them to a stranger with custody of three half-grown children who can offer nothing more than a houseful of beat-up furniture and a trip to the mountains for the weekend. If you are a son and are introducing your parents to your bride-to-be and her four children, they may accuse her of wanting to marry you for your money so that she and her children will be cared for. In their eyes, you are going to be nothing but a meal ticket!

Suddenly your parents begin to feel that their family tree is beginning to bear unfamiliar fruit, as they attempt to deal with unforeseen and sudden changes in their world. For some grandparents this is relatively easy, but others have great difficulty adjusting to the changes. Their support of you and your decisions may be extremely helpful during this period of planning for remarriage and stepfamily adjustment.

Your parents may be pleased with your plans and your new family and at the same time have many conflicting feelings within themselves and therefore sometimes seem unsupportive when you least expect it. For instance, one woman, upon learning that her son was getting married to a woman with five children, accepted the situation gracefully and generously. Privately, however, she said that she didn't feel old enough to be a grandmother, that it was very confusing to suddenly have five strange young children underfoot on the weekends, and that answering to the call of "Granny" or "Grandma" was rather unnerving!

Being cut off from grandchildren

Because of different custody and visitation arrangements, grandparents, like stepfamilies, fall into many different types and categories. For example, you may have custody of your children so they see their grandparents as before; or your ex-spouse may have custody of your children and express anger at you and your parents by making it difficult for your children to continue the warm relationship with their grandparents that they previously enjoyed; or your parents may have become instant stepgrandparents—just as you have become an instant stepparent.

Unfortunately, many grandparents who would like to continue to see their grandchildren are suddenly cut off from having contact with them, and in such a situation both grandparents and grandchildren suffer. We talked to a woman with custody of her children who had married a man without custody of his children, who lived with their mother a hundred miles away. The children's mother made it clear that the children's paternal grandparents were not welcome to either come to see them there or have the children come to visit with them. This meant that the only times the children could see their grandparents were when they were with their father and stepmother, but the father's ex-spouse would seldom permit such visits. Consequently, the children were cut off not only from their father but also from their paternal grandparents. The fact that the grandparents had had a close relationship with their grandchildren before their son's divorce made this a particularly painful situation for everyone. In this stepfamily, the grandparents were very accepting of their new stepgrandchildren, but for the stepfamily there was sadness mixed with caring, because, at family gatherings the grandparents, the children's father, his parents, and his new wife were constantly reminded that some of the children were missing from the new stepfamily.

Even when they are not yet cut off from their grandchildren, grandparents sometimes fear that a remarriage of their grandchildren's parent will mean a permanent loss of contact for them. In their fear they enter the custody arena ready to fight for their child and his or her children, producing even more conflict and tension between the divorced individuals or at times between the newly married couple.

There are a number of ways that you, as the parent of the grandchildren, can reduce their fear of loss and be helpful to the grandparents of the children in your stepfamily:

1. Arrange times that grandparents and grandchildren can do things together as they may have done before your remarriage.
2. Arrange times for stepgrandparents and stepgrandchildren to have the opportunity to get to know one another—starting out with short visits together. They might go to a movie or a swim meet together or go to the store for some forgotten groceries plus a small treat.
3. Arrange times for all the children or a "mixture" of step-siblings to be with their grandparents/stepgrandparents for longer visits once the ice is broken.
4. Include your parents in some of your new family's special events.
5. From time to time include your parents and your spouse in adult activities which all of you enjoy.
6. When possible, make opportunities for the two sets of "in-laws" to get to know one another.
7. If there are "family heirlooms" which you feel your parents would like to have go to particular family members, talk to them about their wishes and plans for legal arrangements. Sometimes grandparents feel strongly about leaving prize pos-

sessions with a family history "in the family." This is understandable and such decisions can usually be explained to the stepgrandchildren so they are comfortable.

8. Do not push your parents to settle money matters and financial inheritance. It usually takes considerable time for grandparents of remarriage to feel comfortable in this area. They often feel strongly about "blood relationships," particularly when the bonds between them and their biological grandchildren considerably pre-date their relationship to their stepgrandchildren. Again, absolute equality in inheritance is not necessary.

9. Be sensitive to the fact that the children's grandparents, just like the rest of the members of your new household, need time to adjust to the family changes that have taken place. Even in very extreme situations, when a remarried adult son or daughter has been disowned or disinherited by a hurt and angry parent, a slow reconciliation may occur over a period of time, as long as the door has been left open for this to happen.

10. As in other stepfamily matters, share these concerns with your spouse so that there can be support for you and together you can work out the best plans for your particular household.

Building bridges or building walls

In most stepfamilies, all the adults and children would like to be accepted by the older generation, and grandparents are in an excellent position to build bridges or build walls between stepfamily members. If they build bridges, it is easier for you and your family; if they build walls, then you and your spouse, and at times the children as well, will need to work together on how best to deal with the situation.

Ways in which grandparents build walls

1. Your new spouse is not welcome in your parents' home

This is a difficult position for the remarried parent who feels caught between his or her parents and new partner. If you are in this situation, consider the difficult position your spouse is in—alone on the outside, with you, your children, and your parents and perhaps other relatives on the inside. If you are the excluded spouse, consider how it hurts your partner not to have parental acceptance of his or her marriage decisions. Mutual support and understanding can help lead to productive discussions on what each of you can do to best handle the situation.

If the difficulty is with your parents, you are probably feeling helpless; however, instead of remaining helpless, pulled in all directions, you can be in a powerful position once you take a firm stand with your parents by making it clear to them that you now have a new partner whom you wish them to acknowledge and welcome.

If you keep attempting to appease your parents, you may stir up anger and resentment between you and your spouse. When you take a strong stand, even though your parents may be angry and upset at first, they may gradually begin to include you and your spouse as a couple. If by any chance it does not work out this way, your couple relationship will nevertheless benefit from your offering support and caring to your partner.

2. Your stepchildren are not welcome in your parents' home

Sometimes parents will accept a new partner, but decline to have any connection with stepgrandchildren. If the children are in their late teens or are young adults, this may not be important. However, if the stepchildren are younger, not being included as part of the stepfamily unit by stepgrandparents usually leads to hurt feelings and jealousy for the children and resentment between you and your spouse.

The feelings involved and the choices to be made are similar to those just outlined when a new spouse is not being accepted—it simply involves more people, a new spouse and children, rather than just a new partner. As with other complicated stepfamily relationships, the ability of the two of you to be supportive to each other insures greater success in working out satisfactory solutions. As before, the major responsibility for "action" usually falls to the spouse whose parents are involved, since this adult is the link between his or her parents and the new stepfamily members.

3. Your new marriage is not
acknowledged in any way

Tony and Janice had been married for ten years. Each had children from a previous marriage. Tom and Tina spent equal time with their mother and their father, Tony, while Janice's two daughters spent all but the summer months with their mother and stepfather. Tony's parents had never accepted his marriage to Janice, and during the ten years there had been very little contact between Tony, his children, and his parents. Then one October a special occasion arose for Tony's parents—their fiftieth wedding anniversary. Fancy invitations were sent out, and one came addressed specifically to only Tony, Tom, and Tina. After ten years of marriage to Janice, Tony's parents were still unable to accept the stepfamily.

Rejections like this unfortunately do happen and cause hurt for everyone involved. If hurt and anger continue to eat into you, it can be helpful to talk with your spouse about the feelings or with others experiencing similar painful family relationships. It also helps to remember that cut-off relationships can occur in any type of family.

4. Your new marriage is being
sabotaged by your parents

In their wish for a return to the family status quo, a few grandparents of remarriage act to put severe strains on the new couple. If your parents become highly upset and threaten to or do "disown" you, or if you find your parents not maintaining contact with you or their grandchildren, it may be that they have the hope or fantasy that you will reverse your decision and return to re-form your original family unit.

Spreading rumors, interpreting things you and your spouse do in hurtful ways, telling your ex-spouse you are not treating their grandchild properly or talking negatively to their grandchildren about you and your new partner are ways in which grandparents, in their frustration and pain, sometimes try to compensate for their feelings of helplessness and regain control of the situation. In such situations, for the sake of your marriage and to protect your children from added loyalty conflicts and more stress, you may need to take firm action:

- Work together as a couple to provide the commitment and stability your family needs.
- Move further away from grandparents psychologically and/or geographically so that family cohesiveness has a chance to develop away from disruptive influences.
- Explain clearly and firmly to the grandparents in the form easiest for you (telephone, letter, in person) that there needs to be cooperation between the adults (both generations) before you will agree to permit their grandchildren to visit them.
- If an ex-spouse is also involved, do what you can to work cooperatively in this matter for the sake of the children. Otherwise the children may get caught in the crossfire between their grandparents and one or both of their biological parents.
- Control what you can control, and remember that relationships shift over the years as strong emotions subside, family coalitions alter due to many unforeseen events, and children mature and go out on their own.

5. Unequal treatment of
grandchildren and
stepgrandchildren

Just as stepparents feel differently about stepchildren than about biological children, particularly in the early stages of their relationship, so do grandparents feel differently about grandchildren and stepgrandchildren. Stepgrandparents may wonder what is expected of them as far as stepgrandchildren are concerned, and if they live at a distance they may have little or no contact with older stepgrandchildren.

If, however, there are two sets of children in your stepfamily, and if the grandparents/stepgrandparents are insensitive to the insecurities one of you may be feeling or to the jealousy between step-siblings not treated equally by them, walls can be built between members of your household.

Birthdays and holidays—particularly Christmas—are times when grandparents frequently are responsible for producing considerable stress by demonstrating their biased feelings openly, thereby hurting their stepgrandchildren and new son- or daughter-in-law. For instance, Bill and Joan had been married for three years and spent Christmas with Bill's parents each year, as had been Bill's custom during his first marriage. Rose, Bill's daughter, was happy to go each year and received many expensive gifts from her grandparents. In contrast, Holly, Joan's daughter, who was similar in age to Rose, received a card and five dollars from her stepgrandparents. Remembering the Christmases of her early childhood, and feeling jealous and depressed as her stepsister Rose opened gift after gift from her grandparents, Holly endured the holiday for two years, but finally she rebelled by refusing to go with the family to Bill's parents for Christmas. This refusal, however, upset Joan because Joan wanted to please her husband and she kept hoping that she and Holly would be accepted by Bill's parents. Joan realized how poorly her daughter was treated in comparison to her stepdaughter, but she tried to make it up to Holly at other times during the year, and she pleaded with Holly to join them all at Bill's parents for Christmas again. Tensions grew between Bill and Joan, as well as between mother and daughter, and between the two girls.

In situations such as above, we have found the following can be helpful:

- Don't expect the children to accept highly "unequal" treatment. As an adult you are able to understand the complexities of the situation in a way the children can't.
- You may find that the grandparents/stepgrandparents will change their behavior if they understand that you don't expect them to *feel* the same about their stepgrandchildren as they do about their grandchildren, but that you would like them to be considerate of the needs of all the children.
- Talk to the children about their grandparents/stepgrandparents and find out what their feelings are. Young children get upset if one gets four presents to the other's one or if one gets a tricycle and the other gets a tiny plastic duck. Older children tend to recognize that grandparents will do more for the grandchildren they have known from birth than for stepgrandchildren, and are content as long as the differences don't blatantly emphasize feelings of being discounted and rejected.
- If the grandparents/stepgrandparents continue to behave so differently towards their stepgrandchildren and their grandchildren

that there is constant turmoil in your family, be alert to the children's feelings and creative in working out holiday plans that don't cause problems in your household. As we've said before, there will probably be no perfect solutions, so confer and pick the best solution that you all can think of—for example, alternate where you have Christmas; have grandparents come to your home for Christmas; take a stepfamily vacation at Christmas; let the children go to their own biological grandparents for Christmas celebrations, Passover, etc.

6. Doting on a new grandchild

When the new couple has a child together, once again there are changes in the stepfamily constellation and in the relationships with grandparents. Sometimes, without even being conscious of it, the grandparents focus all their love and attention on the new little one, while the older grandchildren and stepgrandchildren are pushed into the background. This often happens after the birth of a baby in *any* family, but in a stepfamily parents and grandparents need to be especially alert to the feelings of the older children.

Jack and Lila Black had been very careful to treat their stepgrandson Joey equally with their grandson Martin. The two boys were both eight and the Blacks realized that it was very important to their son that they accept his new wife Jill and her son Joey. Indeed, the Blacks and the Winters, Jill's parents, enjoyed each other and spent numerous evenings playing bridge together.

Then little Karen was born! She was a little doll, with her grandfather Winter's dark hair and eyes and her grandmother Black's high cheekbones and dimpled chin. The grandparents could talk of no one else and lavished clothes and toys as well as attention on the new baby.

Joey and Martin felt somewhat insecure with the birth of their new half-sibling because they realized that the baby had a blood relationship with all the adults, parents and grandparents alike. The behavior of the grandparents fanned the flames of jealousy. No one realized what was going on until Joey's and Martin's school counseler called to say that Joey was hitting other children and becoming a behavior problem, while Martin, in contrast, was withdrawing, daydreaming in class, and not finishing his school work.

The older boys were attracting attention in negative ways. They did need the attention of their grandparents and stepgrandparents. The adults were confused at first, and then they got the message. The adult couples began to take steps to once again create some attention balance within the household, and Martin and Joey not only settled down, but also enjoyed the playfulness of their little half-sister, becoming very protective and admiring "older brothers."

If the negative spiral has already started, take a look at the situation from your spouse's viewpoint and put yourself in his or her children's shoes. Then work out together, as a couple, a renewed relationship between you and make clear to your parents the importance of including all the children in your stepfamily in their lives. If your parents are unable to include both the new grandchild and the stepgrandchildren in their affections, then you will need to make different arrangements —for example, separate visits with their stepgrandchildren at one time and their new grandchild at another time, or being present and taking an active role yourselves in the activities to balance the inequalities.

Ways in which grandparents build bridges

1. Stepgrandparents are important to their stepgrandchildren

Grandparents can be very important people to their grandchildren and stepgrandchildren. They can supply love and fun that tired parents can't always give, and they can supply for stepchildren a non-threatening link to their stepparent. Children are used to having more than one set of grandparents and so another set or two doesn't make life seem so different as far as grandparents go. For this reason children tend not to feel the loyalty conflicts that come with a new "mother figure" or "father figure." This means that grandparents/stepgrand-parents, or stepgrandparents who are not also grandparents, are in a very special position in a stepfamily. Often, stepchildren relate easily and warmly to their stepgrandparents long before they can accept their stepparent. This means that, if you are a stepparent, your stepchildren may enjoy doing things with your parents before they are able to relax and begin to relate warmly to you or you to them. This is one way for your stepchildren to get to know you—through knowing your parents, their stepgrandparents.

One particular situation in stepfamilies, however, is more complicated—when stepgrandparents suddenly become grandparents for the first time. If you have been a stepparent with no children, then your parents have been stepgrandparents only. When you have a child, your parents now are grandparents, as well as stepgrandparents. At this point, unfortunately, your parents may be swept up with joy over the infant grandchildren, who may look like them and whom they've known from "day one." Their stepgrandchildren may suddenly disappear as far as they are concerned. If this happens, not only can your stepchildren feel hurt and angry, but your spouse may feel a "rejection" of his or her children by your parents as a personal rejection also. Your couple relationship could begin to wobble. Instead of enjoying this exciting time as the two of you had anticipated, more and more arguments may develop, and hurt and anger pile up.

If you are aware of this possibility even before the birth of your baby, you will be in a position to talk to your parents about the need the older children will still have for them and thus guard against their becoming "doting" grandparents and uncaring stepgrandparents.

2. Learning how your stepfamily
wishes to relate to them

When stepgrandparents are suddenly faced with a new son- or daughter-in-law and stepgrandchildren, they may feel confused. There are so many new people all at once; they wonder what spot the new family wants them to fill. One remarried mother talked to her new in-laws, telling them just how she'd like them to relate to her children. This opened communication channels right away. For many grandparents/stepgrandparents a heart-to-heart talk can give them a feeling of being important to the family. They may not want to babysit your children every other day or look forward to feeding your cat and watering the lawn while you take a month's vacation, but getting to know one another and discussing how children/stepchildren, parents/stepparents, and grandparents/stepgrandparents are going to fit together comfortably is a good way to start relating.

3. Doing "fun" things with all
the children

One grandparent couple had always taken two of their four grand-children on a special trip during Easter vacation time—the two girls one year, the two boys the next year. Suddenly they acquired two stepgrandchildren. Now they had more children to visit with them, so they added an extra trip during Christmas or summer vacations. At time siblings went on trips with the grandparents; at other times step-siblings came—Dickie and his stepbrother Mike one time, Florence and her stepsister Laura another time. The children had fun and new alliances formed. In this way these grandparents/stepgrandparents helped the members in the stepfamily to become more integrated and more comfortable with all their new relations.

4. Creating new family traditions
for your stepfamily

While you may be developing new traditions in your household, your parents also have the opportunity to create new traditions which include themselves as well as your new household. Perhaps you will need to suggest how much fun it would be to spend a weekend on their farm with them, or go with them to their cabin in the woods, or have a barbecue some Sunday evening in the summer. Feeling included and important to all of you helps grandparents/stepgrandparents become comfortable and they in turn may think of many ways of doing special little things for the children.

5. Being a safe place in a storm
for the children

Grandparents and stepgrandparents can become a safe and cozy spot for your children when they are feeling upset. Even if they live at a distance, if the children have had an opportunity to get to know your parents or your partner's parents, they may often use the telephone or write out their feelings in a letter. "Grandpa Joe" and "Grandma Jill" will understand and won't be upset or take sides—they are somewhat removed and can sometimes be more objective and less involved confidants for a child who is reaching out for someone who understands. For the children in your stepfamily this is an important gift indeed.

At times it may be difficult for you to see your children or stepchildren turning to your parents rather than to you. Try to accept this behavior as a valuable "grandparent function" (as it is in all types of families) and so don't think that there is anything "wrong" with you as a parent or stepparent because this is happening. Because of the added complexities in a stepfamily, having older people to turn to can be particularly important for the children and may also relieve you from an unnecessary emotional burden. Indeed, getting rid of some emotional tension through talking to grandparents and stepgrandparents can free your children and stepchildren to develop warmer relationships in your household.

6. Supporting the adults in your family

The support and acceptance of one's parents are things that "children" of any age, six to 60, wish for. You may have met with disapproval from friends and neighbors as you divorced and remarried after your divorce or after the death of your former spouse: "It was too soon to remarry," "Imagine taking in a woman with five children!", "How can you do this to your children?" may be some of the remarks you heard. You may still feel these barbs—and more besides: "He's not treating your children right," "You sure are mean to your stepkids," "What are you fussing about—you knew what you were getting into."

Your parents can be a steady support in times like these. Their understanding and emotional giving can act as a lifeline for the whole family. Many grandparents of remarriage are very supportive as they deal with the changes in their lives and in the lives of their children and grandchildren. They don't take sides. They nourish and support all the stepfamily members. They stay out of the middle, but are there when needed. In these and in many other ways they contribute their special talents and wisdom to the newer, as well as to the older, members of the family.

Just as children want approval from their parents, so parents of all ages want appreciation and acceptance from their children. Your parents need your support as you in turn need theirs. Working together can make it easier to build welcome bridges to a bright today and a brighter tomorrow.

8 | Legal Issues

Custody and visitation matters

Custody and visitation agreements are basic and important parts of a divorce agreement where children are involved. With the increasing numbers of families having to deal with divorce, combined with rapid changes in American society, the legal system is facing difficult challenges. There is even a growing sentiment among attorneys that custody and visitation issues belong in the counselor's office rather than in the courtroom!

Until the beginning of this century, judges had few custody agreements to decide. Divorce was uncommon and when it did occur children were considered the legal property of the father and were subject to the laws of inheritance and property ownership; custody was awarded almost automatically to the father. There was a change when

American families began to move from farms to form small and then larger cities. Mothers began to be considered the primary caretaker with responsibility for caring for the home and children. The previous system was "reformed" and custody of the children began to be automatically awarded to the mother unless it could be proved in court that she was an obviously "unfit" person.

Further changes have been taking place during the past 20 years with the blurring and overlapping of male and female role expectations and the awareness that fathers also play an extremely important part in their children's growth and development. Which parent is awarded custody of the children is no longer an automatic matter. Now judges increasingly recognize the importance of the decisions they are making and their impact on the welfare of the child and they are looking for help in making these often complex decisions. Counselors and therapists are being employed in Family Court or Conciliation Court offices to advise the judge regarding custody and visitation decisions.

More and more judges and attorneys, as well as divorcing parents, are asking such questions as: "What will happen if Joseph stays with his father and Martha lives with her mother? Is it all right to separate the children like that?" "How long should a two-year-old visit with her father?" "What will happen if my ex-wife and her new husband move to another state and I can't get together with my children every other weekend?" "What will happen if Lena goes to live with her father and stepmother after living with me for the seven years since the divorce?" "What is 'joint custody' and does it really work? Doesn't it confuse a child to keep going back and forth between two homes?"

You may have often asked yourself or others such questions. Unfortunately, at this time we do not have the answers, based on good research, to all of these questions. In the next few years we expect there will be more and better information available as a result of studies which are going on right now and these results will become available in the professional and popular literature. But even now there are some helpful guidelines:

- Except in a few situations, children grow and mature more easily and satisfactorily if they maintain some regular contact with both of their biological parents.

- Children up to the age of three seem to need a sense of continuity with a primary caretaker in their lives. They have difficulty adjusting to several different parental figures. For example, it might be harmful to two-year-old David if he spent one week receiving his care from one parent and then was moved to another home and parent for a similar period of time. Visits with the other parent should probably be of a few hours, or a day's duration rather than a few days' duration. (Baby-sitters and day-care are okay as long as there is one primary care person who is in charge most of the time.)

- After the age of three, children can begin to spend longer times away from their primary caretaker. This means that "visitation" patterns may change as children grow older. For example, eight-year-old Sara spends her school year with her mother and stepfather and half her summer vacations with her father and stepmother, who live in a different state. If it is not too expensive, it would be helpful if Sara could keep in touch with her other household by phone when she needs to; otherwise, letters can be exchanged. It is important for Sara to feel that she has two homes where she is loved and wanted and that she does not have to wipe one of them out of her mind when she is at the other.

- It is very upsetting for most children to be asked to "choose" with whom they want to "live." Even during the teen years having to make such a choice can stir many deep conflicts and loyalty issues, but children of this age are better able than younger children to handle such a decision because they are growing more independent, their peers are becoming very important to them and they are beginning to figure out what kind of adults they want to be.

- Some parents are good with young children, while other parents deal more effectively with older children. Thus, a change of custody as a child grows older at times can prove beneficial for both adults and children if such a change is desired. One 25-year-old young man spoke of his earlier years, "I think I had the best of both worlds. Before the divorce I had my father who was great with young boys and not so good with older kids, and then in my teens I lived with my mother and stepfather, and he was good with teenagers and uncomfortable with little children." Children's needs change and parenting skills change.

- Children usually need to know what the plans are going to be—what is going to happen to them. If they don't know, they can feel very scared and unhappy. Naturally, when they are little, they don't want to know for the next year—just for the next week or the next month. Two of the most frequent questions a child secretly or openly asks are: "Where do I belong?" and "What is going to happen to me?" You need to anticipate these often unspoken thoughts and provide answers.

- If at all possible, keep from arguing with your ex-spouse about custody and visitation issues, particularly in front of the children. Adults and children alike suffer when these matters are the subject of frequent angry discussions, especially when the battle continues in the courtroom. Basically, everyone loses emotionally, no matter what the final court decision turns out to be.

At one meeting where lawyers, judges, parents and mental health professionals were present, ". . . at one highly emotional point in the proceedings, a number of parents who had been involved in child-custody disputes in the courts revealed how, after spending thousands of dollars on attorney fees, they finally escaped financial and emotional destruction and succeeded in resolving their differences only with the assistance of professionals outside the legal system. With tears and cheers, the audience gave them a standing ovation" (*California State Bar Journal*, March 1980, p. 132). An increasing number of attorneys agree that custody and visitation is a counseling rather than a legal issue. Try to talk it out and not battle it out. Then use a sensitive attorney or a mediation court to help you get your wishes written out clearly and satisfactorily. If you can't agree with your ex-spouse, the judge will decide—but the final decision may not be as good as one you could have worked out for yourselves.

One couple found that when the ex-spouses could not find a solution and both families were miserable, their two new spouses, the two stepparents, were able to make contact and negotiate a satisfactory solution for all concerned. "Their meeting lasted four hours. Concessions were made, some of them dealing with finances and some with visitation rights. . . . There is nothing legally bonding about their arrangement. And, as one parent said, 'The agreement probably wouldn't hold up in court, we know that, but . . . we're willing to do more to make it work because we know that people who really care were behind it' . . . " (*San Francisco Chronicle*, August 30, 1980, p. 11).

Fathers without custody

Although more and more fathers are receiving custody of their children, the highest figure we have heard is that only ten percent of divorced fathers have custody of their children.

If you are a father without custody, you are probably feeling guilty that you have caused pain to your children by your divorce, even if you were not the one who wanted the divorce. You may also be feeling guilty that you don't see your children as often as you think you "should" or as often as they want to see you. Or your ex-wife may be accusing you of letting the children down by not doing more for them and being with them more.

Sometimes talking with other fathers in similar situations can be helpful. By feeling less guilty, you can feel less pressured to see your children and you will enjoy the time with them much more when you *do* get together. You may even find that as things go more smoothly you actually enjoy spending more time with them.

Another very common feeling expressed by men who do not have custody of their children is a tremendous sense of helplessness. You may feel that you can have very little or no input into, or control of, your children's lives. Further, if they are living with their mother in a household where they also have a stepfather, you may feel useless and unnecessary. In such situations, these feelings, together with painful times together and painful good-byes, may lead you to pull away more and more from your children until you have little or no contact with them.

Do your best not to cut yourself off from your children! Although it is difficult to visit them with the sense of helplessness and the pain of loss running through you, your children will benefit from continuing contact with you, and as they grow older your relationship may, as it often does, grow easier and less painful when they are more on their own. No other man can take your place with your children. You have your own individual gifts to give your children—your sense of humor perhaps, your skill at fixing things, your interest in stamp collecting, or your simply being there to let them know they are human beings who are lovable and cared about by you.

If you have stepchildren and do not have custody of your children,

> Keeping even minimal contact between adults and children can lead to future satisfaction since time and maturity bring many changes. With some communication among stepfamily members, satisfying interpersonal relationships often develop in the future when children become more independent in their relationships with both biological parents and with stepparents.

your feelings of helplessness and pain when you think about your own children may lead you to resent relating to your stepchildren and doing things for them or caring about them. One man in this situation said, "Everytime I read a bedtime story to Nancy I think about Terrie and feel angry that she's not there to hear the story too." Or as another remarried father said, "I resent driving Mark to baseball practice and sitting and watching him play, when I can't do the same thing for my own boys."

Remember that you will always remain an important figure to your biological children, and at the same time your stepchildren need your caring too. You probably have plenty of love for all the children who need you. You need not feel that you are taking something away from your own children when you relate to your stepchildren.

Mothers without custody

Until recently it was fathers who "left home." Now mothers also sometimes "leave home." The movie of Kramer vs. Kramer only focused on one aspect of the little boy's relationship to his mother and father. It is clear, however, that when the mother left her husband and child, it was not because she did not love her son. Many women in our changing society leave their children—because they feel worn out and emotionally drained, or because they see the parenting skills of the children's father as equal to their own and have a need to pursue a new path for a while, or because they love their children and see the children as having more opportunities to form a closer bond with their father after a divorce. In other instances, mothers protect their children from the pain of court battles by agreeing to custody arrangements at variance with the arrangements that Americans have come to view as traditional.

Mothers without custody of their children have all the same feelings of helplessness, guilt and resentment towards stepchildren that fathers without custody express. In addition, if you are a mother without custody of your children, you may have an added feeling that your friends and neighbors are wondering what is wrong with you. You yourself may wonder if you are a bad mother because you don't have your children with you. Our society seems to expect women to take care of their children no matter what—anyone who is different from that pattern is suspect. As the patterns of society change and more children remain with their fathers after a divorce, such feelings may occur less frequently.

If you don't have custody of your children, you will probably be asked many tactful and not-so-tactful questions by friends and relatives. Doubts about yourself and your worth as a mother and as a person can start to undermine your self-confidence. Loss of self-confidence and feelings of worthlessness are very devastating. If you do have those feelings and can't shake them, try reading books on co-parenting or talking with other mothers without custody of their children. It can also be very helpful to talk with a counselor who is familiar with the problems of people in one of the many new family patterns and arrangements that are emerging in America today.

If you have remarried and having stepchildren causes you to want custody of your children, or if you find yourself wanting to resume parenting your biological children, remember that frequent custody changes are difficult for children. Perhaps you can work out alternative ways of relating to your children without a change of custody. A mediator might be very helpful in this situation—one who can see the whole picture and give you suggestions for ways to meet your needs in ways that will also be supportive for your children.

Joint custody

Joint legal custody means that both biological parents retain input into important decisions regarding the life of their children. While joint custody certainly is not the answer to soothing all the ruffled feelings of parents and stepparents, it does reduce a sense of helplessness for many parents, and gives them a specified and important role to perform in regards to their children. What areas are to be included in such decisions are worked out in advance by the biological parents. For many separated couples, having a third neutral person present can be most helpful, although it is possible to work out arrangements on your own if you are on good terms with your ex-spouse.

You might include the following as items to be decided by input from both you and your ex-spouse:

1. Where will the children live, and for what lengths of time?
2. What schools will the children attend?
3. How will important elective, as well as emergency, medical care be obtained?
4. What summer activities (i.e., day-care, camps) will the children participate in?
5. What extracurricular activities will be provided and by whom?
6. Who will be responsible for the financial support and insurance arrangements?

Joint legal custody does not mean that children live equal amounts of time with each parent. Your children's ages, your working arrangements and geographic constraints will all play a part in these decisions. To cite one situation, it could be detrimental to three-year-old Charlie to spend a year with his mother and stepfather in Washington and the alternate year with his father and stepmother in Colorado. At such a young age Charlie needs to have homes geographically close so he can see both parents frequently, or have one home in which he spends the majority of his time, while being with his other parent for short periods of time. Three-year-olds cannot understand major shifts in living arrangements as can older children, nor can they hold on to relationships in their heads and hearts over a long period of absence from an individual. They need the stability of one caretaking person and, at the same time, frequent contacts with their other biological parent, if possible. Sometimes geographical distance and financial considerations make frequent visits difficult or impossible. In such cases, phone calls, cards and letters can substitute for personal contacts.

One little four-year-old whose father had not visited him for over a year talked to his father by telephone each month and danced with excitement whenever he received a can of maple syrup made in the town where his father lived. This contact was enough, but if his father's communication fell below this level Timmy became depressed.

If you and your former spouse live close together, then the types of living arrangements are much easier to arrange. Going back and forth between your two homes takes little travel effort, and your working schedules can be easily considered in deciding where the children will be during what time periods. For example, if both you and your spouse are working fulltime outside of your home, and your children's other household has a mother or stepmother there who is at home most of the time, then it may work more successfully for your children to spend time in your home when you and your spouse are relatively free and not working, and in their other household at the other times. One six-year-old girl, living most of the time with her father and stepmother and their little girl and with her mother during the times her mother was not working, felt secure enough with this arrangement and with the amicable relationships she saw among the three parenting adults in her life to say unconcernedly to her father and stepmother one day, "If the two of you get divorced, then I'll have three homes!"

We heard an 11-year-old talking recently about his living arrangements. His father had remarried, his mother had not, and Donald spoke of loving his mother, father, and stepmother. The two households were only blocks apart, and he spent Mondays and Wednesdays with his father and stepmother, and Tuesdays and Thursdays with his mother. Fridays, Saturdays and Sundays went together and they were alternated between his two households—one weekend with his mother, the next with his father and stepmother. Donald also spoke of enjoying special events in each household, but said he didn't want to do things with all three adults together because sometimes his mother and father argued with each other when they were together. Despite their differences, these three adults had worked together to create an environment in which Donald felt cared about and secure. He was unconcerned with the frequency of the shifts. In his mind they were very clearly spelled out.

Children are able to adjust well to many situations if they know what to expect, feel wanted and see that it is okay with all the adults to accept the rules, regulations and pleasures of each household.

For many parents and children joint custody works very well because it says clearly that both parents are important to their children and that the children are indeed important to each of their parents. For parents in single-parent households it also relieves some of the heavy emotional burden that can accompany having to carry full family responsibility alone. In addition, research indicates that joint custody insures that more fathers stay involved and connected with their children—something that is very important for all of you.

One recent book dealing with parenting and custody considerations that you might find helpful is: *Mom's House, Dad's House* by Isolina Ricci.

Visitation arrangements

One of the generally unrecognized problems that individuals in stepfamilies deal with is the effect of negative images coming from the words that are used to describe different aspects of stepfamily living—negative terms like "broken homes," "unfit parents," "wicked stepmother," "cruel stepfathers," "poor neglected stepchildren," "unsuitable marriage material" (remarried adults). Also included are the words used in this chapter which are words also used to apply to prisoners—custody and visitation.

At the present time there seems to be no term other than "custody" to describe the legal decision, but even though we speak of "visitation" and "visitation rights," you can change your thinking to view the matter not as "visitation" or "visiting children," but to how long and when your children will be living with you or living with your former spouse. If your children think of themselves as having two households and "living" in each of them, even if it is only for two weekends a month or a week in the summer, it says to your children that they belong in both places and are not "visitors." You have different expectations of guests and visitors than you do of household or family members, and treating your children or stepchildren as "visitors" or "guests" usually does not lead to stepfamily harmony.

In drawing up legal agreements, the term "visitation" continues to be used and "visitation rights" are usually spelled out, often in great detail. Unfortunately, contracts can be commitments to try to defeat, to alter, to push to the limits, and so on. Your children will be happier —and therefore you and your household will be happier—if you do not make "visitation" a fighting issue between you and your ex-spouse. When you really feel emotionally "separated" from your former partner so that you don't carry around a huge load of anger or guilt, then you can probably "trade off" and work out flexible "visitation" arrangements, although all involved adults know what it says in the legal agreement.

The major point which we keep stressing, however, is that children need to know what the plans *are*, and as they grow older they need to have increasing input into what the plans are going to *be*.

- Two-year-olds need to be told just when they will be with Mommy and with Daddy.
- Five-year-olds need to have the same information, and they also like to know what enjoyable things are being planned. At this age, doing errands with a parent can be fun, as well as buying an ice cream cone, having a special bedtime story, and so on.
- Ten-year-olds plan further ahead, and want to have some say in the plans. If Jan's best friend is having a birthday party, she wants to see that "visitation" plans won't prevent her from being at the party.
- Teenagers are shifting from wanting to do things with their "family" to wanting to be with their peers. They often plan several weeks or months ahead, and they may rebel and provoke difficulties if they do not have a say in the plans or are forced to be somewhere against their will. At this stage of development custody is sometimes changed to the advantage of everyone or the amount of time spent in each household may be altered or reversed even though there is no formal change of custody. This can often work out very well as long as switching back and forth is not permitted every time the adolescent gets angry with the regulations of the present household.

Many parents complain about the lack of spontaneity they feel in making stepfamily plans. In most cases it is true that you cannot suddenly decide to take all your children and stepchildren to the beach for a picnic because the sun has come out and it's a beautiful day. More people are involved in your type of family—your children's other parent and his or her plans—or several sets of grandparents and plans they may have made. This may not be your weekend for all members of your household to be together.

It is often frustrating to bump up against this "visitation wall." However, you, as well as your ex-spouse and the children, need to know those limits, for they also make it possible for you to count on times you can plan to do things you'd like to do together. This may not be your weekend to all be together, and therefore a trip to the beach for all of you is not a possibility. But your turn will come. And also, if you don't get yourself stuck in an angry spot dwelling on the limitations of your weekend, you will be able to think about the choices you *do* have —to do something alone, or as a couple, or with a child or two, depending on your particular wishes of those who *are* with you. And that can be a lot of fun!

If you have children or stepchildren who are with you all or nearly all of the time, you won't have to deal with as many transitions as occur when the number of members in the household keeps changing. This does add a sense of stability to your household that can make for easier routines and planning. Even in this situation, however, we have found that it is very important for the children to have written or telephone contact, however minimal, with their other parent or, if their other parent has died, to feel free to include that parent in their memories and in their lives through pictures and special belongings. Roots and a sense of heritage are a fundamental and deep need for everyone.

Adoption

Stepfathers very often adopt their stepchildren and stepmothers sometimes adopt their stepchildren. When stepfathers adopt this gives all members of the household the same last name, which is at times one reason for the adoption. Adoption, however, is a legal cutting of biological ties, and as such requires very careful consideration. Fortunately, society is becoming conscious of stepfamilies and the differences in last names. Adolescents report that different names do not cause them much stress, and schools are learning to ask if a child's last name is the same as that of his or her parent. Much more awareness is needed, but it is slowly growing!

We are often asked about the positive and negative effects of adoption of a stepchild. Again, this is an uncharted area and some serious study of the effects of adoption needs to be done. We do know that adoption is not the answer if you are thinking that by adopting a minor stepchild you will be doing something to improve your relationship with this stepchild. Your day-to-day interaction, acceptance and enjoyment of each other are what will determine your relationship.

When the other parent has died

One situation in which you may want to consider carefully the wish to adopt your stepchild is if your stepchild is very young and his or her other parent has died. Adoption in this case will give you legal rights to have a continuing relationship with your stepchild if your spouse should die or if in the future you and your present partner were to separate or divorce. Since at present there is no legal relationship between stepparent and stepchild, there are times when stepparents, stepchildren, and step-siblings are cut off from each other and lose very important relationships because of a divorce or the death of a biological parent. If your stepchildren are older, they may consider adoption a rejection of their parent who has died, and this means that any movement in this direction would need to be gradual and include open discussion with the children.

When the other parent is alive

Minor children ordinarily cannot be legally adopted without the consent of both biological parents, unless one parent has disappeared completely. Often children are asked in court if they want to be adopted, not knowing exactly what is meant. Even if they "feel" the meaning of the question they often answer in a way they think will insure them a more secure place in at least one household. For example, ten-year-old Jane spent most of her time with her mother and stepfather, though she was with her father and stepmother for some weekends and parts of longer school vacations. Jane was asked in court if she wanted to be adopted by her stepfather. She said, "Yes," and since her father, who was also present, did not object, the adoption was accomplished. In her twenties Jane could look back to that day and remember the conflicts and the fears she had felt. She had *not* wanted to be adopted, and thus be legally cut off from her father, but she felt unwanted by her stepmother and also by her father, and she felt a strong pull from her mother for her to say "Yes." Jane feared that saying "No" would make her mother angry, and then she would have no household to belong to. So she said "Yes."

Adoption creates rights and responsibilities, but it does not create relationships. Your ex-spouse may do little to indicate any desire for a relationship with your children and yet refuse to give permission for adoption. For many people a sense of personal continuity and immortality comes from having children bearing their genes and family heritage. Cutting off parents from the next generation or cutting off children from those biological roots requires very careful consideration, even when the other biological parent agrees to the adoption. To your child the other parent's willingness may be felt as deep rejection even though you, your ex-spouse and your present spouse may see the adoption as the creation of a stronger and more cohesive family unit. Some adopted stepchildren have never known their other biological parent because that parent left when the child was a few months old; later they often seek to find their other parent or change their name back to their birth name despite many years of happiness in the family in which they grew up.

Adoption may simply be an attempt to return to square one and become a "nuclear family" because the adults continue to use the nuclear family as the ideal model for a family. There is simply more than one type of satisfactory family pattern. Much needs to be explored in this area of adoption but it seems clear that adoption is not the answer to stepfamily problems and in no way insures a cohesive, happy, adoptive family. Indeed, the comment has been made that a person who would be willing to adopt his or her stepchildren would ordinarily be willing to work on good stepparent-stepchild relationships in any event.

If you are thinking of adoption in your stepfamily, we strongly suggest that you talk to a counselor familiar with different types of families and adoption complexities before making a final decision.

Money arrangements

Remarriage has been referred to as sexual monogamy and financial polygamy! Financial agreements made at the time of your or your spouse's divorce may seem totally unreasonable to you now, and discontent and anger over money can push you and your present spouse into opposite corners of the room! One attorney entitled his talk on alimony and child support, "Too much is not enough." Neither party feels satisfied.

Bob felt he was paying his ex-wife Josie too much money now that she was working—and besides he had no control over what she did with the money. Josie felt that she deserved every penny she got and more, after all those years of keeping house and raising three children; also, in her anger she kept telling the children that she couldn't take them to the movies or buy them special treats because their father was stingy and didn't give her enough money. And Marty, Bob's second wife, felt that all the money she earned somehow went to support Josie and Bob's children, and that she and Bob didn't have enough left to have any fun together—all the extra had to go to pay for child support and expensive birthday and Christmas presents.

There are many reasons why money can be a "hot" issue in stepfamilies:

1. With so many more individuals involved and with child support and alimony, there is often a lowered standard of living for everyone concerned.
2. Men who have been divorced may feel they were "taken to the cleaners" by their previous spouse, and so are hesitant to let their present wife know anything about their financial status or financial affairs.
3. Women who have been divorced and found themselves totally ignorant of financial matters may have become financially knowledgeable and competent during their single-parent household phase and do not wish to return to their position of financial dependency.
4. Women who have worked and been independent for a number of years may wish to keep this sense of monetary independence.

5. Money paid to or by an ex-spouse is a continuing tie to the former spouse and can feel to the new partner like an emotional as well as a financial commitment to the former family unit. New wives who work outside the home often comment, "All the money I earn simply goes to support my husband's ex-wife and her household."

6. Grandparents of the children may be concerned about inheritance issues and act in divisive ways that tend to split the stepfamily.

Trust between you and your spouse is necessary to work out money issues in a smooth manner. Because of the reasons just listed it may take some time for the two of you to be comfortable in this area. After painful experiences it takes time for trust to build. Money may be a subject to touch only lightly until you find yourselves working together well in other areas.

Here are some of the ways that couples in stepfamilies have *unsuccessfully* worked out their monetary issues:

1. Each remarried parent has paid for himself or herself and his or her children's expenses. This has created two separate families living under one roof. If there is a large difference in personal assets, one group in the house may have plush vacations and closets full of clothes, while the other group camps out at a local ranch and has half-empty closets. You can imagine the jealousies that arise!

2. Because of a deep sense of guilt and fear of not seeing his children, the husband has continued to give his ex-wife money over and above that required by the divorce agreement, which reduces his available income so that his present household has little or no money for small luxuries and recreation. The feelings of "unfairness" can make for many major arguments between the new partners.

3. Because his stepchildren have received lavish gifts and trips from their father, the stepfather feels devalued and insecure. He withdraws from the family, thus denying himself, his wife and the children in his new household the pleasures they could have had getting to know one another and having pleasant times together.

4. The remarried mother insists on staying in the house she and her children have been living in, and she refuses to put her new husband's name on the deed to the house. Her husband continues to feel like an outsider and, except for the easy chair he brought with him and squeezed into the corner of the family room, he has no spot that he can call his own.

There are many unhappy variations on these four themes, but let's look at creative ways stepfamilies have managed their financial affairs to insure a sense of security and comfort:

1. The spouses discuss their past experiences with money. If they find that they have very different approaches to handling money, they think about compromises and even write them down. As trust develops, they put money both into a joint account for household and family expenses and into separate personal accounts for special personal needs and wishes.
2. The spouses keep their accounts separate and each pays for himself/herself and his/her children, but they talk together when necessary to insure that all members of the household can go on vacations together and receive similar allowances for clothes and money for hobbies and lessons.
3. Where the trips and gifts given by an ex-spouse to his or her children are extravagant, the adults decide together, sometimes in consultation with the ex-spouse, how to work out ways in which jealousies within the household unit can be minimized. Often children in the family can accept the differences better than the adults can, particularly if the gifts are seen as simply being a parent's way of being part of his or her particular child's life now that he or she has little day-to-day contact.
4. The couple puts all money into "a common pot" and uses it for the stepfamily as needed.
5. As the children reach 18 years of age, educational or other "child support," if any, may be paid directly to the children. In some families some of the child support funds are paid directly to a child, starting at age 16 to 17, for personal use (clothes, recreation, etc.), although some still goes to the custodial parent for living expenses connected with the children (rent, food, utilities).
6. Where major family changes have taken place, such as loss of a job, illness, a large inheritance, etc., monetary arrangements are

discussed and changed either informally by consent of the adults involved or more formally by having a new legal agreement executed.

Misuse of custody, visitation and money

Custody, visitation and money are areas of major overlap between the children's two households. As a result, if hostility, guilt or confusion remains, these areas become magnets for difficulty. When this happens, children usually suffer even more than the adults, as they bounce back and forth between warring parents. Child support payments are not sent on time, custody battles drag through the courts and visitation is sabotaged, as angry ex-spouses exercise their power to disrupt as a way of expressing their feelings.

Give your children the support they need by staying out of such battles and avoiding such annoying behavior. Take out your mad feelings by talking to others in the same boat or to friends or counselors who are neutral and understanding. (But remember that friends can only listen so long before they begin to feel helpless to do anything to make you feel better.) Think about all the things you *can* control and make yourself feel better. Relax your expectations. There are no perfect solutions. You owe it to yourself and your family to concentrate on the good things in your life so that your mad feelings won't eat you up. Take advantage of pleasant opportunities that come your way and roll with the ship when the seas are rough—you will feel less seasick that way. And besides, a beautiful coastline may suddenly loom up ahead.

9 | Helping Children Adjust

There are many ways in which parents and stepparents can help their children and stepchildren adjust to the myriad of changes taking place in their lives. Some have to do with learning communication skills, others have to do with following practical suggestions and still others have to do with having realistic expectations of yourself, your partner and the children. And some have to do with a belief in yourself and the sense of mastery that information and knowledge can give you. All these things can lead to your increased enjoyment of your new family and to greater satisfaction with the changes on the part of other family members. Reading and taking classes in parenting and child development, as well as classes and workshops for stepparents and remarried parents can be helpful. Also, organizations for stepfamilies are developing local chapters. Joining such a group can be very supportive.

Children who live with you most
or all of the time

When the children live with you for long periods of time, you can work out living arrangements that are more stable than if your family expands and contracts frequently. You may feel more relaxed about working out new family patterns because there is plenty of time to do it; besides, you may have a sense that you can be an influence in the children's lives because they are with you most or all of the time.

If there are also children who join your household for shorter periods of time, it is difficult not to treat them as "guests" and have the children who are already in your home feel "unspecial" and neglected. Here are a few ways to avoid stirring up such feelings in the children already living with you:

1. Do "special" things from time to time whether "all" the children are with you or not. In this way it is not Disneyland weekend and six chocolate sundaes only when the "visiting" children are with you.
2. Consider "visiting" children as simply *living* with you for shorter periods of time. This makes them truly part of the household and not "guests" in their minds and in your thoughts too. This means they will then share in the household chores and activities that accompany having more people around, as well as in the special games, talks and recreational activities of your family. If they are treated as "guests," the children who live with you for longer periods may feel jealous that the "guest" children aren't asked to fit into the usual pattern of the household—in fact, sometimes the children in the household feel they have to act as hosts or even servants to the "visiting guests."
3. As much as possible, let the lives of the children living with you remain unaltered when the household expands. For example, do not ask them to share their toys or rooms or to go without their Little League practice, unless it is a change they wish to make. Space can be a problem; if rooms must be shared, give the children as much say as possible in how this is to be done. Children come up with some very creative ideas!—a trundle bed tucked away under another bed, a sewing room or office easily converted into an extra bedroom, or bunk beds that often help children

band together because having both beds occupied seems special and lots of fun, particularly if they enjoy talking together as they are settling down and growing sleepier and sleepier.

4. Communicate with the children. One stepmother had an experience in which she suddenly found herself being shifted so that she had to join an already existing group. She immediately felt isolated, angry, and very uncomfortable. That evening when she went home she told her 11- and 12-year-old stepchildren that she could understand that it must have been very hard for them to suddenly be told they would be living in her household, and she could understand their feeling very mad about it. The 11-year-old looked at her with some disbelief and exploded, "It was the pits!", and the 12-year-old began to open up and talk to his stepmother for the first time. A dialogue and a relationship had both started at the same time.

"Visiting" children

We know that "visiting" is the familiar way of referring to children who are with you for short periods of time, children who seem less "permanent" members of the household. However, we wish to repeat that thinking of them as simply "living" with you for whatever times they are with you can put everyone in a different frame of mind. They *do* have a parent in your household, and therefore are members of the household. Often children are considered to be "visiting" because their other parent has custody of them, while children are considered to be "live-in" children in the homes where they are with their custodial parent. Many times, however, children's living patterns change with no accompanying custody changes. Additionally, the legal terms are cold and inflexible—the same ones are used to refer to the strong arm of the law coming out and grabbing someone, taking them into custody and setting "visitation" rights. Because of this, many individuals are working to change the legal system to work more sensitively with divorce and remarriage issues and do away with these negative, legalistic words. However, you don't need the legal changes to change your way of thinking about children who live with you for short periods of time.

"Visiting" children usually feel strange and are outsiders in the neighborhood. It can be helpful if they have some place in the household that is their own, i.e., a drawer or a shelf for toys and clothes. If they are included in stepfamily chores and projects when they are with the stepfamily they tend to feel more connected to the group. Bringing a friend with them to share the visit and having some active adult participation in becoming integrated into the neighborhood can make a difference to many visiting children. Knowing ahead of time that there is going to be an interesting activity, stepfamily game of Monopoly, etc., can sometimes give visiting children a pleasant activity to anticipate.

Noncustodial parents and stepparents often are concerned because they have so little time to transmit their values to visiting children. Since children tend to resist concerted efforts by the adults to instill stepfamily ideals during each visit, it is comforting to parents and stepparents to learn that the examples of behavior and relationships simply observed in the household can affect choices made by all the children later in their lives when they are grown and on their own.

Nevertheless, when children are with you for a short period of time, there are certain feelings and situations that may arise.

1. Because of your desire to influence the children's lives in ways you consider beneficial, you may feel under pressure to do so in a big hurry because you have so little time to do it—a few weekends, a year, a few weeks in the summer or a couple of adolescent years since they are 16 or 17 and about to be on their own. Pressuring another individual of any age usually makes that person angry and resistant, and so what you want to get across is rejected and everyone feels frustrated. Simply being with you, having a relaxed time and seeing how you approach life and do things have much more effect on the children than you can ever imagine from their outward response! Indeed, your influence can also continue during the years when the "children" are grown and on

their own, very often becoming evident many months or years later in the way they handle situations.

It is true that the children may not choose life patterns you would wish for them. This happens, of course, in any type of family. Removing from your shoulders the burden of trying desperately in a short period of time to mold partly grown individuals the way you wish them to be can make you feel more relaxed. With the pressure off, everyone can have a happier time together. As one teenage stepchild said, "I think one big problem is that the adults have an idea in their heads about how the children ought to be and then try to make them fit that pattern. The more they try, the more determined I am not to change."

2. Children who are not with you a great deal of the time wonder if there really is a place for them. You can help a great deal in seeing that there is indeed a place:

- Be sure toys, games, etc. belonging to those children are always in your home and are kept in a spot of *their own* that is not touched unless permission is given by the owner.

- Do not consider them as "guests." At the other extreme, do not use all your time together to get a million chores accomplished. Being part of the household happens in many ways. One stepmother who married the man with whom she'd been living for some years said the marriage had made such a difference to the children. As she put it, there was more turmoil at first. The second or third weekend after the wedding, her children and her husband's daughter, who was with them for the weekend, got into a big hassle. Then the two adults started to become involved in it too. "So I found then that I took my stepdaughter, May, away from the others into a room by ourselves and said to her very directly and clearly, and with deep feeling, 'May, you're my stepdaughter now and you have a place in this home!' " The stepmother went on to say that she realized she was really saying to May that because she *did* have a place, she had the right to fight with the others, be listened to, not be considered in any way an outsider—so she had to get in there and stick up for herself. May did, and after that there weren't even any fights!

It seems to us that May's stepmother was also making it clear that being a stepmother was perfectly fine and that being a stepdaughter was no lesser a position than being a daughter. Equality within the household is important.

- Have clothes, toothbrushes and the other necessary daily items remain at your home in a space provided so that children do not need to arrive, as guests do, toting such items along with them.
- Introduce the children to others in the neighborhood, making it easy for them to overcome initial uncomfortable periods—perhaps by taking neighbors along to a movie or on a picnic, or inviting them to make popcorn with your family.
- Allow the "visiting" child to invite a friend along on trips or to spend the weekend with your family. A familiar face can relieve you of having to "entertain" in ways that may be necessary if the child who is with you isn't yet secure in your household and neighborhood. Indeed, friends can be welcome additions at any time.

If there are only two adults in your household most of the time and then there is one child living with you for a period, a threesome may be difficult to manage comfortably. One person often feels left out, for only two people can really have eye contact and relate directly to each other (try it—you can't look at two people at once unless their faces are only inches apart!). Many "threesome" stepfamilies have reported that taking a friend of the child's with them camping or simply inviting the friend to stay for a weekend has turned tense, unhappy times into pleasant occasions for all—the children relate to each other and the adult couple then has time to be together and not feel the necessity of entertaining that third little individual.

One threesome stepfamily in which the husband's child was with them nearly all of the time could not, of course, have a constant boarder-friend. Father and daughter did some things together; stepmother and stepdaughter did some things together. Even so, particularly at meals, it was hard to keep the attention balanced when all three were together. Tensions grew until one day the stepmother shared *her* feelings of being left out with her stepdaughter and said she imagined her stepdaughter felt the same way sometimes. There was a nod of the head and the beginning of a real friendship as adult and child talked for a short time about how that does happen with three people. Each felt understood, and that was helpful.

- Be available, but don't force a relationship. Let the children, particularly older ones, help figure out what kind of "place" they want to have in your household.

Transition periods

For most people transitions are difficult because any change involves giving up something. Leaving school is exciting but also unsettling as you wonder when you will see your friends again; changing jobs may be a challenge you want and at the same time there can be a sadness as familiar places and people are not seen as often. Visiting with friends, you may feel strained at first until an initial strangeness wears off. And if you have mixed feelings about change or don't want the change, then the transition is even more difficult and painful.

Children changing from one household to another usually feel tension, as do all the adults involved. In a movie of a stepfamily, the father whose children have come for the weekend to be with him, his wife and his stepchildren talks about the typical disruption at "both ends," arguments as the group gets together on Friday evening and hassles with some withdrawal as people contemplate splitting apart into two groups again as the weekend together draws to a close. As he says, it's painful for him and he's sure it is for the others as well.

If you will remember that these unsettling periods are time-limited, then they become predictable and easier to handle. Children and adults will "settle in" just as you do when you change from work to home or from your home to a friend's home for a party, so hang loose and let the grumpiness or rudeness at these transition times pass by as no big deal.

Being "handed over" from one household to the other, or arriving on your own when you are older, can be difficult for many children, as well as for the adults involved. Loyalty conflicts, jealousy, anger and fear often surface at these times. If you have worked these transitions out well with all of the adults, you are probably finding that the children manage the times without any real upset. However, this can be a stressful period and you may want to give some thought to making changes if the children seem tense or unhappy. Here are a few suggestions to start you thinking about possibilities for your household:

- Break the transition for the children so they don't go immediately from one household to the other. For example, perhaps they can be picked up at school by the family with whom they will be spending the night, weekend or next few days. Or perhaps you can meet them for hamburgers before returning to your household. The idea is to choose some neutral territory for meeting and thus reduce sudden emotional transitions.

- If many angry and upset feelings still remain between ex-spouses, stepparents can often deal with their partner's ex-spouse more easily. If so, then the adults from each household who can best work together to plan the comings and goings of the children may be the ones to do it—cooperative planning removes a certain amount of tension!
- Some stepparents feel that they need to be at the front door to greet the children even though they feel uncomfortable because the children are young and so "brought" to the door rather than coming in from the car or bus alone or bicycling themselves. Tenseness doesn't help anyone, so it may be easier to remain elsewhere in the house for these few moments. Then the transition may be smoother.
- Sometimes it is the remarried parent who feels the greatest discomfort around the arrival of his or her children. In these situations, then, it may be the stepparent who can best open the door and greet the people standing there.
- If the ex-spouses are uncomfortable together, reducing the amount of contact when the children come to your home or you take them to their other household is, of course, a good idea. It's mighty uncomfortable to chat civilly at the door or sit and have a cup of coffee together when you're preoccupied with a load of upsetting emotions tumbling around inside you. The children will probably react better if it's a short exchange, particularly if they have been told in words or clear behavior what to expect.
- When there's a big difference between what is expected and what actually happens, children and adults get upset. For this reason, be sure that the adults have worked out ahead of time any changes in how transitions are to take place. If you're expecting a 15-minute conversation in the living room over a cup of tea and instead you get a "Hi and good-bye" and the door closed in your face, you can experience a lot of anger and frustration!
- In an attempt to work out these transition times, remarried parents often seek to reduce tension by having their children do the arranging with their other parent. For teenage children this may work at times, but too often making arrangements this way puts the children in the middle, giving them a power they both like and don't want at the same time.

If you can't talk in person or on the telephone, you can still make arrangements with your children's other parent by writing notes.

Children often stir the pot by landing on your doorstep and telling you what a terrible time they've had in their other household or the reverse—what a simply glorious time they've had. Often they are telling you what they think you want to hear or, if they are angry at you, they may be telling you just what they think you *don't* want to hear. You can help them adjust by not swallowing hook, line and sinker what they are saying, particularly if you feel they are trying to engage you in some kind of argument. Sometimes it is difficult to accept that children *can* have good times in each of their households doing very different things, which may cost very different amounts of money. It can be fun to travel, go skiing or go on a shopping spree. Perhaps you can't afford these luxuries or don't enjoy such activities. It is also very pleasant for a child to bake cookies or read a favorite book with a parent. What really makes a fundamental difference in the lives of children now and in their future is having the experience of being cared about and listened to. Having your favorite cereal on the shelf and your best buddy spend the night with you often means more than flying to Sun Valley to ski and being emotionally ignored.

Loss of contact with one parent

Losing contact with a parent either through death of that parent or after a divorce is for many children one of the deepest and most painful experiences in their lives. Even when the parent has died before the child's birth or when the child was only a few months old, the loss may still leave its mark. Years later people may feel cheated by life and sense that something very important is missing. They may be strongly driven to find out all that they can learn about their heritage, their roots. One man whose father died when he was less than six months of age was adopted by his stepfather as a baby and grew up in a happy family. Nevertheless, he chose to use his biological name when he came of age, rather than his stepfather's. This act did not signify any loss of love for the parents he had known and loved all his life—it simply satisfied a very deep need for a feeling of personal identity.

After the death of a parent, children often react in ways puzzling to adults. Instead of crying and being sad, they may seem non-reactive and casual about it all. This is their way of dealing with a very deep loss or, if they are very young, it may simply mean that they are not yet old enough to emotionally grasp the finality of the loss. Whatever their reactions, children are helped by knowing that their relatives and remaining parent are very upset. Even if the marital relationship has been poor, death stirs much sadness, and attempting to shield children from these appropriate emotions exposes them to an unfortunate model for their own emotional well-being. Boys and girls, men and women need to laugh when life is funny and cry when life is sad. This is part of being human. Even when the death is very sad and tragic, children can learn to accept the loss of a parent, though they may need much support and perhaps professional help.

More complicated, however, are the reactions of children to a parent who has "disappeared" from their lives. Except in cases of somewhat severe physical or mental abuse, most children want to retain some form of contact with both biological parents. Seven-year-old Timmy saw his father only once a year and talked to him on the telephone only occasionally. Timmy seemed happy with these arrangements. However, recently his father missed his yearly visit and he has not telephoned Timmy for a number of months. Timmy is asking his mother more and more about his Dad; frequently, he becomes very upset and misbehaves at home and in school. Timmy's mother has been making excuses for her ex-husband's behavior, but she now realizes that she needs to help her son talk directly to his father, perhaps by helping him write a letter or initiate a telephone conversation, so that Timmy's father will know how his son feels and hopefully respond by continuing the contact.

If you have children in your household who have no contact with their other parent, you may want to help them establish some contact if this is possible. If it is not possible, or if their other parent rejects the contact, then the children may have the following reactions:

1. They may become depressed because of the rejection by someone who has a very important personal meaning to them.
2. They may feel that there is something wrong with them and that they are unlovable.

3. They may withdraw from you and other family members because of their feelings of hurt and anger.
4. They may start misbehaving and acting in antisocial ways, in a few cases to the point of lying, stealing and getting into trouble with the law. Delinquent behavior or severe school difficulties often signal the need for professional assistance.

Sometimes parents have felt that it would be a help to their children if they slowly made less contact possible with their other parent. At times parents have even moved away leaving no forwarding address and giving their children the impression that their other parent no longer cared about them. If this has been true for you, you may want to reduce your children's feelings of loss and sadness, or anger, guilt and reduced self-esteem by helping them get in touch with their other parent.

When the disappearance is something you have not wished and may yourself feel angry about, it will be hard to help your children because of your own anger. It can really help you in the long run, however, if you don't blast off to your children about their other parent, because if you do you may have a more upset household to deal with.

If possible, the main help you can be to children who have lost a parent in this way is to respect and understand their feelings of sadness and anger, although you need not accept their destructive ways of getting rid of their angry feelings. Talk to the children about how upsetting the situation must be for them. You can also (at a later time) tell them clearly that the actions of their other parent have to do with something going on inside that other adult—and that it is *not* a message that the children are bad or unlovable children.

At such times stepparents sometimes try to step in and take the absent parent's place. This can really backfire! Children do need added parenting from stepparents in such instances, but they still resist attempts to replace or somehow "take away" their other parent.

Rivalry and fighting between the children

Because a stepfamily is more complex, the chances for competition and arguments are increased. One group of children may feel that the other group is favored. When Joannie goes off to be with her father,

Tad and Jason may feel jealous because they are staying home with their mother and stepfather and "nothing's going on this weekend"; or Jim and Laura fight because Jim says his stepfather is nicer to Laura than he is to Jim. The combinations go on and on depending on the kind of stepfamily pattern you have. Here are some suggestions on handling rivalry and competition:

- Take a load off yourself by remembering that children in nearly all families, whatever the type of family it is, have many disagreements between them. Whenever possible, let them solve the problem without getting in the middle. If you do find they need your help, do your best to remain neutral and listen to both sides. Sometimes when the feelings are expressed and heard, then workable solutions follow.

  For example, Ronda and Paul were having a battle royal because Paul yelled at Ronda that she had taken some of his baseball cards. "No, I didn't!" "Yes, you did . . ." and on and on. The fight got worse and Ronda's mother decided she would need to help them calm down. She gave them a time-out for ten minutes (going to their rooms not as punishment but to cool off some) and then she sat down with them to discuss the matter.

  Even after ten minutes the "discussion" was hot rather than cool, but the mother managed to ask questions and listen to the feelings of both children. Slowly the feelings of anger began to lessen and practical suggestions made by Paul's stepmother were heard by both children and they themselves came up with ideas about where the missing cards might be—and off they went together to look for them. This time the story had a happy ending because Paul found the cards had slipped down behind his bed where he'd been playing with them the day before!

- Try to be fair to stepchildren and children alike, and ask your relatives to do the same. Many children know that *they* feel differently about their parents and stepparents, and so they can understand and accept that stepparents and stepgrandparents may feel differently from parents and grandparents. However, if you have three aunts and like one a lot more than the other two, you may consciously see that you treat them equally at Christmas, send each a birthday card and visit with each one of them from time to time. The same kind of consideration toward all the children in your stepfamily can help reduce the jealousies and disharmony between them.

- Have the same general expectations of behavior for your own children as you do for your stepchildren. If it's okay for your children to leave hair in the bathroom sink and dirty clothes on their bedroom floor, then it needs to be okay for your stepchildren to do the same. If not, you may have mutiny on your hands!
- Stick together as a couple in dealing with the children; otherwise they may try to split the two of you and draw up sides. It's hard not to fall into this trap because of your special feelings about the children you raised from birth, but if you and your partner are drawn into opposing camps you may have more than mutiny—you may have civil war!
- Think about the needs and wishes of each child separately. Being fair does not mean giving everyone a ten-speed bike the same year. Perhaps one child wants roller skates and another a bright red wagon. The dollar amounts may be different—it's the feeling of receiving what *you* want that makes for equality. Some children like to talk to you a lot, others don't; some need to take part in athletics after school, others like to come home and read. Being accepted for what you are and what you like feels good and fair—and therefore the children will feel that they are cared about and there will be fewer jealousies and fewer ruffled feelings and noisy arguments.

New children in the family

Just as having children together tends to hold first marriage partners together, it appears that having children together may tend to hold a second marriage together. What happens, of course, will depend a great deal on your response and your spouse's response to differences in feelings at having an "ours." So before talking about how older children in a stepfamily react to a new baby joining the household, let us consider the feelings of the adults.

Deciding whether or not to have a child together causes much concern and conflict in marriages where there are already children from a previous marriage. This seems to be particularly true if one spouse has not already had children. If you both have children, you are both parents and stepparents and you have had similar experiences in terms of having been parents. Perhaps you want more children or perhaps you don't. Obviously, if one of you does and the other doesn't, the issue needs to be discussed. (The same issue comes up in first marriages where there are no children and one of the spouses wants children and the other one does not want to have children.)

If, however, you are a stepparent only, you may want a child of your own—but at the same time you may have many reservations. Your partner may have three children and feel that's quite enough, or you may wonder if you really *do* want a child because you find the experience of being a stepparent not especially rewarding or even downright difficult. You ask yourself if being a parent is the same. Particularly if your spouse isn't enthusiastic about adding another child to the household, you may go back and forth between wanting a baby and not wanting a baby. This is such an important matter that the two of you may want to talk with a professional counselor to help you with your decision.

If you do have a child, so that you become a parent as well as a stepparent, you will have to make special efforts to show that you care about all the children in your stepfamily. Being a parent for the first time can be a deeply moving experience and the feelings may be very different from the feelings you have about the cute little five-year-old you have stepparented for the past two years. It is difficult not to become so emotionally involved with your new baby that your spouse and his or her children feel cast aside. Your spouse needs to know you still care about his or her children or else your involvement with the baby can feel like a personal rejection not only of the children but also of your marriage partner. Having a child *and* continuing to care deeply about all the stepfamily members can create a truly joyous feeling within the whole family.

We hear over and over again from stepfamilies where the adults work out the new family relationships well and the children in the family respond with sheer delight and enthusiasm to the new arrival. Often the arrival of this helpless little creature, who begins to respond and coo and smile at the children already in the family and who is actually blood-related in part to all the other children, creates a feeling of relatedness and integration in the household. As in any type of family, this unity grows as long as the older children do not feel pushed out and neglected by the new arrival. Include the older children in caring for a new baby to the extent that they are capable and enjoy the responsibility and you may soon find that the little one finds a place in everyone's heart.

Sexuality in stepfamily households

The children in your stepfamily probably find your household much more sexually stimulating than the other households they remember. You and your partner are trying to have a honeymoon, perhaps, in the middle of a group of children! No doubt the two of you show more affection towards each other than the children saw in the family that split up. As a couple you may not have been alone together very much, and your strong feelings for one another are being picked up by the children. In first marriage families children tend to take the affection between their parents for granted and not really think of them as being sexually involved with each other. And, of course, where there has been fighting preceding a divorce, the children have frequently seen an absence of any affection.

If you have teenagers of different sexes who have suddenly found themselves living under the same roof, you may find them avoiding each other like the plague to push away any sexual attraction. In addition, sexual attraction towards a new person, the stepparent, can also occur, or conversely attraction of the stepparent towards a stepchild. Two quotes from young adult stepchildren looking back illustrate their feelings very well:

> For me, adolescence and stepfamilyhood came at the same time. . . . I suspect I was responding in part to a sense of intrusion. As a developing, but terribly naive young woman, I was in the position of sharing intimate living quarters with a strange male (my stepfather), and then for awhile with a strange male peer (my stepbrother). I felt uncomfortable with the violation of my privacy and anxious about the closeness to men. . . . Given my naivete, I didn't conceptualize to myself that sexual issues were playing a part in my uneasiness.

> I was always thinking about girls and I was always thinking about sex. And one of my fantasy objects was my stepsister. This

was particularly tough because I felt both attracted to women and afraid of women, and there she was in various stages of undress. Whether she actually was or not I really don't remember. I was attracted to her and I was curious about her both as an individual and as a symbol. She was too close to ignore. I couldn't distance from her in that house.

Another one of my objects was my stepmother. And that was even worse! It was even more threatening to me because I was attracted to her sexually and I went out to her emotionally too. There was a lot there in my head. Really my fear about my sexual feelings about my stepmother kept me from expressing some of my positive emotions towards her.*

Because these situations are particularly difficult, we are often asked by the adults in stepfamilies how to deal with the added sexuality in the household. Here are a few suggestions:

1. Children need to see and experience a tender and loving relationship between the adult couple in their stepfamily. However, as adults you can dampen things down a little when the children are around. The two of you can be affectionate and tender with each other without being passionate when the children are with you. Teenagers are particularly sensitive to open affection because of their own emerging sexuality. If you have adolescents, be aware of this sensitivity and "cool it" if you are in the habit of long embraces and kissing in the kitchen.
2. Because you, your spouse and the children have not grown up as a family together, you need to be aware of not being sexually provocative to the children. Going around in undershorts or bra and panties is not the way to keep sexuality under control in your household, even with younger children. Even a slip with no robe can be stimulating and set off inner sexual stirrings in your children, which they may try to control by withdrawal or behavior calculated to create distance by making you angry.
3. "Rough-housing" with young children can be fun, but as children reach age 10 or 11 it can turn into pseudo-rough-housing

---

*From E. B. Visher and J. S. Visher, *Stepfamilies: A Guide to Working with Stepparents and Stepchildren*, New York: Brunner/Mazel, 1979, p. 177.

> Sexuality is usually more apparent in stepfamilies because of the new couple relationship, and because children may suddenly be living with other children with whom they have not grown up. Also there are not the usual incest taboos operating. It is important for the children to receive affection and to be aware of tenderness between the couple, but it may also be important for the couple to minimize to some extent the sexual aspects of the household and to help the children understand and accept but not act on their sexual attractions to one another or to the adults.

and become more a physical turn-on between step-siblings of different sexes, or between stepmother and stepson, or stepfather and stepdaughter.

4. Sons sometimes compete with their fathers or stepfathers for the attention of the woman in the household, and daughters very often compete with their mothers or stepmothers for attention and affection from the man in the household. While it is cozy to cuddle small children and hold them on your lap, resisting the advances of children of 10 or 11 on up can be important. Many a story is told of how 12-year-old Suzy comes to spend the weekend with her father and stepmother, showers her father with kisses and all kinds of coy attention and wants to sit on his lap, while her stepmother spends the time cooking dinner, washing dishes and building up to the boiling point. Work together with your partner so this sort of thing doesn't happen in your home. If you don't discourage such behavior, the end result may be distance between you and your spouse, which can then lead to even more closeness between adult and child in a descending spiral!

5. If you feel that the teenaged step-siblings in your household are having "crushes" on each other, talk with them openly about how such feelings are to be expected when you haven't grown up together and you are suddenly living under the same roof with someone close to your age who is new and different. And make it clear that there is a big difference between *feelings* and *behavior*. Just because you are attracted to someone doesn't

mean you sleep with that person, any more than being angry at someone means that you hit him or her over the head with a baseball bat.

6. Attractions between stepparents and adolescent or young adult stepchildren certainly do occur, again because of the instant new living arrangements. Often, too, the young person is somewhat of a younger version of the man or woman you love and have married. So when you and your partner are having an argument or there is some emotional distance between you for some reason, it is sometimes comforting to turn for emotional support to the younger person. Instead of letting that happen, keep the lines of communication open between you and your partner and the feelings of attraction that often exist will not be overly strong—thus disturbing positive, loving stepfamily relationships.

7. Rearrangement of living space can cool off a sexual situation between stepsiblings. One family, noting the attraction between his son and her daughter, decided to turn a study at the other end of the hall into an attractive room for the daughter, so that their bedrooms would not be adjoining. They also rearranged the bathroom-sharing with another child. A potential problem was solved with ingenuity and the expenditure of a few dollars for re-decorating.

8. Teenagers in stepfamilies often engage in their own provocative behavior, i.e., parading around the house scantily and inappropriately clad. One stepmother with a 13-year-old daughter in the household had reached the limit as her stepson descended the stairs dressed only in his revealing jockey shorts. With great sternness she said, "Go back upstairs and get dressed properly, and don't ever walk around the house in this manner again." The young man angrily obeyed—but he did not repeat the behavior. No doubt he had been asking for someone to set a limit, and it was important to respond by doing so.

9. In some stepfamilies the young people do become sexually involved. Their ages, the feelings of the adults, and the relationships within the household will help you decide what you want to do in such situations. You may not be able to change the relationship between the young adults, but you can decide what is permissible in your household. In one family the adults asked the college-age son to move out of the house since they were un-

willing to accept his sexual relationship with his stepsister, particularly if it took place within their house. As with older children coming from any type of family, what young adults do on their own is something you as a parent or stepparent cannot control, although you can influence what happens in your territory. Occasionally, step-siblings who have met one another as young adults do continue their close relationships and marry each other later on.

10. In all types of families, adults at times turn to their children or stepchildren for emotional support and affection. In some families the relationship may become one of adult-child sexual involvement producing ultimate unhappiness for the family. Remarried mothers of teenage daughters often fear that their husbands will become involved in this way with their daughters.

If you are a remarried mother with this fear, you may be reacting to tales and experiences from your past. Be sure these fears don't get in the way of having a good emotional relationship with your husband. Having a good adult-adult relationship is of primary importance in keeping the sexual bond between the couple, and insuring caring but clearly nonsexual relationships between the adults and children in the household. This is very important.

Growing up and leaving home

Adolescence is a time when children are caught in a conflictual set of feelings—they want to be independent and on their own and at the same time they feel scared about giving up all the familiar supports they have had. Parents and stepparents also are worried and want to protect their children from all the "mistakes" they themselves have made and are sure the children are going to make.

In any type of family, growing up, finding out who you want to be and setting out on your own are hard and at times disturbing tasks.

If there have been tensions between adolescent stepchildren and their stepparent in your household, you may feel that the teenager's rebelliousness, desire to be alone or with friends and lack of interest in stepfamily activities result from unsatisfactory step-relationships. Then guilt sets in, and you may find yourself pressuring for family outings and for some signs of caring from the teenagers. You may make a concerted effort to force them into talking about what is bothering them so you can be sure they don't leave home because of poor interpersonal relationships. This pressure almost never works in any family.

It is true that teenage stepchildren do withdraw sometimes from both their parents at the time of a divorce and start out on their own sooner than teenagers in other types of families. They do not wish to form new adult-child relationships because they may be hurting and angry and wanting to become independent. So they leave sooner emotionally—and perhaps physically too. Or often they go to live with their other parent to get other ideas to try out as they search for their own identity and individuality.

Remarried parents and stepparents, even more than parents in other kinds of families, feel that the adolescent is pulling out because of what the adults have done that displeased the young person. If you fall into this trap, your teenager has a marvelous way to leave and yet not really grow up emotionally—by moving out, blaming everything on you and your partner, or on your ex-spouse, being angry and pushing all your guilt buttons so that you will bail him or her out of the crises of daily living that will occur when he or she is first on his or her own. Be there, leave the door open and try not to panic, because adolescents don't really disappear into the great blue yonder never to reappear again. At the same time, don't make excuses for their behavior, blaming your divorce or remarriage for everything that goes wrong. Most adolescents return for an adult-adult relationship when they feel that they have discovered what they want for themselves and are ready to relate on an independent basis.

Counseling

Parenting or stepparenting is a learned skill. You are not born with it. And dealing with complex stepfamily situations can become extremely draining and more than just an exciting challenge. Your self-esteem and sense of worth may disappear beneath a cloud of discouragement and anger. To top it off, everyone in your stepfamily probably started off with very strong feelings like the ones we have talked about throughout this book, and some of these feelings may still exist.

When you have strong emotions boiling inside of you, it is scarcely possible to even be aware of how others are feeling. So here you all are, wanting to be understood, perhaps feeling angry or guilty, or unappreciated and rejected, and there are so many feelings going the rounds with everyone that there's no understanding or encouragement or support!

Perhaps you have tried some of the ideas suggested in this book as well as many solutions of your own. Often they have worked and your family has settled down. On the other hand, it may be that there are still areas that need attention. We believe that certain situations are particularly difficult in stepfamilies: mourning losses, dealing with hostile parents and ex-spouses, negotiating major differences, working out discipline problems, settling disputes over money, and helping children who are showing a great deal of upset at home or at school.

Every person needs support and understanding so that he or she can handle the tasks at hand. Growing into adulthood and growing as an adult so that you are able to form an intimate relationship with another adult is not an easy task. There may be many traumatic experiences along the way, including death, divorce, remarriage, serious accidents and rejection by peers. And raising children can be a series of trial-and-error experiences, full of unwelcome surprises as well as deep satisfactions, fun and emotional warmth.

Some individuals work their way along the path with little outside help, while others find help in reading, taking courses, and joining groups designed to meet their particular needs. Many times you can save yourself, your children and your family much unnecessary turmoil by talking with a professional counselor or therapist, minister or rabbi, or a family doctor who can help you all clarify your goals, learn to communicate more easily, examine your expectations of yourself and others and help you with the specific areas of difficulty we have mentioned.

Some people view seeking help outside the family as a sign of personal failure. On the contrary, we know how much it can help in troubled times, and we see it as a positive decision to maximize your strengths so that you and your family can gain a sense of personal worth and mastery, thus making it possible to work out complicated stepfamily relationships. You can thus create the satisfactions, enjoyment and feelings of interpersonal warmth that you would like to have.

10 | Emotional Transitions from Previous Households to an Integrated Stepfamily

New stepfamilies are families in transition from former households to integrated stepfamily households. As a rule, the adults in step-families believe the adjustment period will take place much more easily and much more quickly than is realistic to expect. Forming new relationships, working out new routines and satisfactory ways of doing things, and dealing with the comings and goings of your children all take considerable time. When your children are young, it usually takes less time than when your children are older and have had more years in other types of households. Research is indicating that from three to five years is an average time for many stepfamilies to feel "settled." Even when people do feel a sense of belonging to your family group, you may find that when holidays, changes of residence, graduations, weddings, and other family-type events take place things will once again feel uncomfortable for a time. This does not mean that some-

169

thing is going wrong; it is simply due to the fact that stepfamily structure is complex and often there are people in several households to be considered.

Emotional stages of stepfamily formation

For the most part, there are feelings and interactions that take place in nearly all stepfamilies. Reading about remarriage and talking to others in similar situations can certainly reduce the intensity of emotions that usually occur, but we find that most adults experience to some degree the emotional stages described by Patricia Papernow.

Although, of course, there can be differences between families in the amount of time and the pattern of stepfamily development, the following description outlines a very typical process:

Initially the adults, and often the children as well, have many wonderful fantasies about what their new stepfamily will be like. Parent and stepparent dream of "one big happy family" and children often have visions of a "new start" in areas in which they have been unsuccessful or unhappy. After the remarriage, such fantasies begin to fade as reality does not match this rosy picture. For example, relationships and caring do not spring into existence immediately since it takes memories of shared times and successful problem-solving to develop such feelings, and children who may have anticipated special relationships with new stepsiblings may find that their older stepbrother does not want to become a basketball instructor, and their younger stepsister does not appreciate all the jokes they tell. In addition, everyone is doing things differently than they are used to, and the new school is no easier than the former one.

Although the family may continue to try to relate as though everything is wonderful, there is a growing tension with anger peeking around the corners. When things go wrong the group splits into former groups, with parent and children sticking together. If you are a stepparent with no children, you can feel very rejected and left out when this happens. These reactions tend to grow stronger, and stepparents feel isolated from "the other group" and start to wonder what is wrong with them that the family is not settling down and feeling happy.

When stepparents recognize—often with the help of understanding friends, a counselor, or through new knowledge of how stepfamilies function—that their wishes for more spousal support and changes in behavior are realistic and necessary, they may begin talking to their partner about their feelings. If this is the state your family has reached, you will probably find that you and your spouse may be having many arguments—particularly about the children. If you are the parent of the children, you may be feeling helpless and pulled in several directions at once, wanting to please your partner and your children and seeing no good way to do either.

The crucial thing at this point is for the two adults to come together as a couple and to both feel as though they are on the same team. This is often "a gut-wrenching thing to do," to quote one remarried father. When the adults do enjoy one another and can work together to solve the problems that arise in the family, steprelations can begin to develop and to flourish, and there may be a resolution in the dealings with the other households that are important to the children. For many stepfamilies, arriving at this point is not a matter of weeks or months, but a matter of several years or more. As these tasks are accomplished, there is an increasing sense of belonging to the new unit, and the individuals experience many family satisfactions.

Making the necessary changes

You may have found creative ways to move your family from one stage to the next. There is no "right" or "wrong" way; however, there are a number of considerations and guidelines that can help the process of family integration. A number of suggestions are found in the publication: *Stepfamilies Stepping Ahead: A Program for Successful Stepfamily Living*, produced and sold by the Stepfamily Association of America, Inc.*

What happens in any family depends on the interactions between the people in the family. As leaders of the family, the adults' actions

*Address: 215 Centennial Mall S., Suite 212, Lincoln, NE 68508

and reactions are especially important. It seems valuable to discuss the role of the parent who has remarried and the role of the stepparent separately because they often are experiencing very different emotions, and in stepfamilies they initially have very different roles in the family as has been discussed in earlier chapters. Of course, it is the relationship that they create that is perhaps the most important single factor in how the family functions.

Roles for remarried parents

Developing the couple relationship

As suggested in the section on emotional stages that take place during the integration process, the development of a good couple relationship is fundamental for satisfactory stepfamily functioning. This relationship has been discussed at the beginning of Chapter 5, and its importance for the children has been stressed. However, the emotions that arise can be most difficult to handle. Recently, a remarried father talked about his struggle to "become a good father" in his remarriage:

> It took me three years. I suddenly realized that my primary loyalty was to my son and not to my wife, and that wasn't good. My guilt for the breakup of my first marriage stood in my way. Finally I was able to give my primary loyalty to my wife and it made all the difference to the family. It's hard to admit, but she'd been more of a parent and a better one to my son than I had, but now I can be a better father and the family is really working well.

If you are a remarried parent and continue to place the needs of your child or children ahead of those of your spouse, you may not be developing a strong couple relationship and the whole family can suffer from this. While it is usually not possible for children to voluntarily give up the unproductive power they have in the household when their parent maintains the alliance with them that existed before the remarriage, they basically need and want a strong adult couple to lean on when they are young and to rely on when they are older. It is really important to your children!

One other way to think about this shift in loyalty is to conceptualize it this way:

1. You begin your life as an individual $\boxed{\text{I}}$
2. You marry and become part of a couple $\boxed{\text{C}}$ $\Big\}$ = $\boxed{\text{I}\,|\,\text{C}\,|\,\text{P}}$
3. You have children and become a parent $\boxed{\text{P}}$

You are divorced or your spouse dies:
the couple drops out, the individual
and the parent role remain ($\boxed{\text{I}\,|\,\text{P}}$).

Then you remarry:
If the couple role gets added at the end ($\boxed{\text{I}\,|\,\text{P}\,|\,\text{C}}$), rather than in the center, family growth can be affected adversely. The original development of life needs to be duplicated:

$$\boxed{\text{I}\,|\,\text{P}\,|\,\text{C}} = \boxed{\text{I}\,|\,\text{C}\,|\,\text{P}}$$

The ICP gives the family stability and time to form new step relationships. Also, children can grow and leave home and become independent adults more easily and satisfactorily when they know that their parent has a fulfilling couple relationship.

Balancing family needs

Because you love your children and have a bond with them, and because you love your new partner and have a bond with him/her, you may feel caught somewhere in the middle between them. You want to help them all be happy and may feel that, try as you will, you are not really able to keep any of them happy. Your spouse feels left out—your children want more of your attention—you feel helpless. Although it may not seem that way, you are in actuality a powerful person in the household because you *do* have a relationship with your children and with your spouse. Because of this you have the power to help or hinder the development of a relationship between your children and their stepparent. You also are cared about by all of them.

Most times it is not possible to meet 100 percent of the needs of all these people who love you, certainly not at the same time. Remarried parents frequently feel pulled on by family members wanting time with them. It is difficult to balance the needs of the family, even though it is crucial to do so, particularly at first. The children are feeling a loss as their parent now gives time to a new partner, and the new person feels deprived because the usual "honeymoon period" is being shared with children.

Planning ahead so that everyone knows when their time will occur can allow people to relax and feel more secure:

> Babs certainly found this to be true. She had felt pulled apart by her daughter and son and husband, all of whom wanted time with her. She was upset with them, particularly with her husband, whom she felt should understand her children's needs and be "grown up" and not expect so much time with her. With help, she came to respect the needs of her husband as well as those of her children. She also recognized her wish for some "alone" time. Instead of continuing to do most things as a family, the four of them planned one-to-one times together. The children needed "alone" time with her and so did her husband. Babs also expressed her need and worked out time for herself to be alone for several hours on the weekends with no family responsibilities. Babs's guilt at not meeting the needs of everyone subsided, the children were happier because they could each count on times they would have 100 percent of their mother's attention (perhaps not as much as they would like, but definitely more than they had before), and Babs joyfully planned for times alone with her husband.

Supporting the stepparent

In addition to what has been said earlier, there are several specific suggestions for ways in which the parent of the children can help the stepparent and stepchildren develop respectful and caring relationships:

• Thank your spouse for things he/she does for your children. While a parent may be rewarded with a winning smile, a whispered "I love you," or a crudely made birthday card, stepparents do not routinely receive such thanks from their stepchildren. Perhaps such recognition will be given in time, but until such a day arrives, it can mean a great deal to your spouse to know that you appreciate him/her for trips to the grocery, carpooling efforts, and financial contributions in the name of high school basketball.

- Treat your children and your stepchildren fairly if you both have children. If both adults have children you may understand the differences in your spouse's feelings towards children you have known since birth and those you are just getting to know well. Although you may feel differently about the children, if all the children are treated in a fair manner, usually they get along together much better and the couple works together more smoothly and positive new relationships are easier to form.

- Require stepchildren to be civil to their stepparent. The stepparent is not in a good position to request this of the children: this limit-setting needs to come from the parent of the children. When this is done sincerely, the children sense clearly their parent's commitment to and support of their stepparent.

- Make room in your relationship for your partner to form a bond with your children. At the same time that you want your spouse and your children to like each other, you may find yourself hanging on to the very close relationship you have had with your children prior to your remarriage. It may make you feel sad to step back a little and allow these new relationships to form, but in the long run everyone can be happier together. Toby's experience illustrates this very well:

Toby was divorced when his daughter Lisa was 10 years old. Several years later he married Rita, a woman who had not been married before. Rita worked hard to get to know Lisa, doing many nice things for her and many fun things with her. Unhappily, Lisa continued to take advantage of her stepmother's kindness and she was often rude and cutting in her remarks to Rita. Toby continued to relate warmly to Lisa at all times even though he felt upset at the lack of caring between Lisa and her step-mother. Rita grew increasingly upset and angry.

One day as the three started to drive together to go skiing, Lisa made a sarcastic remark to Rita. To Rita and Lisa's surprise, Toby stopped the car and said very earnestly and with obvious emo-tion, "Lisa, it hurts me very much when you speak to Rita that way. She cares about you and I love you both very much and you do this to Rita quite often. It makes me feel very sad." Toby later realized that for the first time he had stepped back a little from his daughter, stood with his wife, and said, in effect, "We are a team." Without his support, there was nothing that Rita was able to say that would alter the situation.

At this point, Lisa began to cry and so did Rita. Then the two women began to talk together, Lisa saying how much she really cared for Rita, but somehow she'd kept pushing her away. From then on their relationship grew and strengthened, and it became very important to both of them. After this Toby also relaxed and was happy with both his daughter and his wife.

Roles for stepparents

Research is indicating that there are many satisfactory roles for stepparents. The fact that the role *is* ambiguous makes for flexibility and for the opportunity to experiment. The important consideration is the negotiation of needs of any particular stepchild and that child's stepparent. The "bottom line" appears to be that the family can function well if the stepparent's role in the family is one that brings satisfaction to the adult and to the child who is involved. This may mean several different roles in the same household depending on the age or needs of the children—for example, a parent role with a young child, a companion of an elementary school-age child, or a mentor and confidante with a teenager. Frequently, stepparents and their spouses believe that a stepparent "should" be a parent. It may be difficult to let go of that expectation and develop a different role, yet it may be crucial to do so.

Supporting the parent

When you have the emotional support of your spouse, it feels as though you are on the same team. This can be difficult to attain in a stepfamily because of the conflicting emotions. You may not like the way the children treat their parent or the way their parent treats the children. You may want different house rules. You may be jealous of the time your partner spends with his/her children. You may feel like an alien because the household rocks along in what seems like a chaotic manner to you. It is very easy to come on like an outside consultant who is present to increase the facility's productivity. It doesn't work! Working *with* your spouse may take much understanding, but it can begin to bring about many of the changes you would like to see take place. The experience and response of Clara illustrates this very well:

Clara, a woman who married a man with three kids who visited them every other weekend said, "I struggled for a year to tell him I wanted some time alone with him while they were here. The weekend was our only time together. He would tell me I was being selfish, and then I'd withdraw and get depressed. Finally, it occurred to me to ask him what it was like *for him* when I asked for time alone. He said he felt incredibly hurt. That he wanted us to be a family, that he had so little time with his kids, and that it felt like I was asking him to disown his children, that I had time with him during the week and why couldn't I let go of him during the weekend?

"Instead of defending myself, for once I *repeated back* what he said to me: that he felt really hurt and maybe scared. You know he started to cry! Something changed after that. It was like we were more on the same team trying to figure out a hard problem: how to give him the time he needed with his kids and still give me and us time alone, together. We came up with this neat idea that the Thursday night before weekends when the kids come, we would have a *date*. When we were poor, it was pizza and watching *Hill Street Blues*. Now we go out to a nice restaurant. We also take at least one walk together while the kids are here. It makes such a difference!" (From "Stepping into Parenting Someone Else's

Children, by Patricia Papernow, in *Making Remarriage Work*, edited by Jeanne Belovitch, 1987,p. 78. Lexington, MA: Lexington Books)

Developing relationships with stepchildren

It has been said that stepparents need "the wisdom of Solomon and the patience of Job." The swirl of emotions usually is fairly constant at first, with pleasurable times with the family increasing as the household settles down. Suggestions for stepparents appear throughout this book. There are also a number of good books written especially for stepparents to help them with their feelings. Several important ones are:

The Good Stepmother: A Practical Guide by Karen Savage and Patricia Adams
Stepmothering—Another Kind of Love by Pearl Ketover Prilik
Stepmotherhood: How to Survive Without Feeling Frustrated, Left Out or Wicked by Cherie Burns
Stepfather by Tony Gorman
Stepfathers: Struggles and Solutions by Charles Somervill

In stepfamilies, the stepparent/stepchild relationships do not develop simply because the partners work well together. They require time and conscious nurturing. However, the two adults are together as a couple because they care about each other. That relationship can bring joy from the beginning. Several times adults have commented that what they wanted was to feel "cherished." The new spousal relationship needs cherishing, as this can make the longer transition to a solid stepfamily unit worth the time and effort it may take you.

Developing a parenting coalition

During the 1960s when the divorce rate began to go up, popular wisdom held that divorced spouses should sever their connections. After all, if they could not get along as husband and wife, fights would erupt if they got together. Since then the impact of divorce on children has been studied and it has been documented that having contact with both parents is very important. As with all situations, there are times when this is not possible or when it is undesirable, but working on preserving these relationships usually benefits everyone. After all, it is easier to live with a happy child. In addition, a working arrangement between parents, rather than an active hostility between them, does much for their emotional well-being.

An increasing number of divorced parents are working out some type of co-parenting relationship now that the value of this has been established. When remarriage takes place, this introduces one or two new adults into the lives of the children. Because they are adults in the household, the stepparents do have some type of "parenting" role, even if it is simply to be a support for the children's parent—a "parental helper" as one stepmother put it.

Since co-parenting usually applies to two adults, we use the term "parenting coalition" to include the three or four adults involved with children after parental remarriage. A coalition is defined as a temporary alliance of separate entities to accomplish a task, in this case the task being to raise the children.

The task of developing a parenting coalition is not emotionally easy—an understatement in most remarriage situations! However, once there is a strongly committed couple, many adults are finding they can accomplish this. It becomes much easier as time passes and is especially useful at the time of special family events such as graduations and weddings. Such a coalition does not signal that adults in the children's two households are friends or that they spend time together. It does mean that the two households are able to cooperate, rather than compete, and that they can be civil to one another. Some couples find it helpful to think of a parenting coalition of three or four adults as a "business arrangement" between the two households.

Developing this type of arrangement has many emotional advantages:

- The adults do not have to carry a load of hostility around and remain on the defensive.
- The children's loyalty conflicts are reduced.
- Children are much more relaxed because they do not have strong fears of saying or doing something that will produce hostility towards one of their households.

- There is help with the responsibility of raising the children.
- Households report much more flexibility around residential arrangements: households are willing to help one another as social or other unanticipated situations arise, rather than having to abide by a rigid schedule.
- Stepparents are included in decisions affecting their lives and this helps them become part of their stepfamily.
- With more adults working out plans there is less opportunity for ex-spouses to return to former negative patterns.
- Having all the adults working together is a clear message to the children (and to the adults) that life has moved on to a new place. No longer is the former couple THE couple as far as the children are concerned.

Stumbling blocks to forming parenting coalitions

While there will be numerous specific deterrents, we are aware of several common difficulties that make it hard for two households to work together.

1. The parent or parent and stepparent in one household fear that the children will want to spend more time in the other household, or that the adults in the other household will try to change the residential arrangements unilaterally. This fear of more loss of time with your children can make you see the children's other household as a threat to you rather than assisting you in child rearing; perhaps the other household has the same fear of your household. If you fear one another, it is not likely that you will be able to work together. Enemies do not cooperate.

   One way of overcoming these fears is to assure your children's other parent (and stepparent if there is one) that you will not change any arrangements without all of the adults in the two households deciding on new arrangements.
2. One or more adults may be "bad-mouthing" another adult to the children. This tears children apart and also hinders the development of any trust between the households. If you find yourself doing this, do your best to control it when the children are

around. (Save it for a support group or a counselor!) If you are the recipient of it, you can sometimes help the children and yourself by saying something similar to what one remarried parent said, "I'm sorry they feel that way about us. They don't live in this house so they don't really know what it's like here." This type of response does not put the other household down, and it gives the children freedom to form their own opinions. If these barbs lose their effect, later you may be able to make a positive comment or help the children's other household in some way that could slowly lead to cooperation. This has happened in a number of households.

3. The parent who has remarried has not yet made it clear that there really is a separation from the former spouse. Having too much contact regarding the children, talking about situations not involving the children, leaving the stepparent out of situations involving him/her (even indirectly), or acquiescing to many unexpected requests from a former spouse may suggest that one or both of the former spouses are having difficulty letting go of the former relationship. It often takes time and is emotionally upsetting to make this type of psychological separation, but until each person in the new couple feels secure in the new unit, it can be upsetting rather than positive to work out a parenting arrangement with the other household.

If you feel insecure in this way, perhaps you can talk to your spouse about it. Sometimes it is helpful to find a counselor to help because this is an area that can be very complicated and painful.

Aids to forming parenting coalitions

Basically, the necessary ingredient to working together across households is having sufficient trust in your spouse and in the other household so that you can count on one another. Many people in stepfamilies are surprised to find that this type of trust can be realized. You can probably think of ways to build trust between your children's households. Here are some ways other stepfamilies have found useful:

- Making positive comments to the adults in the other household. For example, "Thank you for taking Johnnie to Little League"; "We appreciated your picking up Alice at school"; "The children really enjoyed the movie you took them to see."
- Letting the other household know when a child has been ill, what the doctor advised, and if there is medicine the child needs to take if he/she is changing households for a few days.
- Meeting with a counselor to work out school and residential arrangements or other matters involving the children. Meeting with a person outside the two family units can serve to reduce the escalation of emotional tension as well as to provide a valuable outside facilitator.

We have learned of many families who find it possible to form such coalitions, even after a number of years of hostility and sabotage. These families also report incredible relief and pleasure in the way the family settles down. In particular, they find that the children have more of a sense of belonging to the new family unit and they appreciate the increased integration in their household.

In summary: Because of their biology and their emotional attachment to both of their parents, your children may be connected to more than one household. It can bring rewards rather than stress when the households cooperate in the raising of the children. The adults have assistance with their parenting responsibilities, and the children have fewer loyalty conflicts and thus it may be easier for them to form caring relationships with their stepparents.

If there is stress between your children's two households, when the two of you have nourished your couple relationship and both feel secure as a parenting team, then you may find that it is possible to respond to your love and caring for your children and stepchildren, as well as to your own tensions, by letting go of past anger and hurt and doing whatever you can to develop a civil relationship with the children's other household. Even if you need outside help to deal with this difficult process it can be well worth the effort. Lessening conflict between households can be a very special gift you give yourselves and your family.

11 | Looking in the Mirror Again

Human beings are complicated, exciting creatures. One of the wonderful things about them is their ability to figure out why things are the way they are. Another wonderful aspect of human beings is their potential for emotional and intellectual change. No longer do people view the world as flat; no longer are sun and rain and thunder the result of the good and evil thoughts and acts of people; and changing rapidly are long-held ideas about racial differences, the value of men and women and the horizons of life in general.

In this book we have been concerned with the changes in families in present-day America. Most people think of the biological family as the "standard" American family and use it as a yardstick by which to measure and judge other types of families.

Just as there are differences among biological families—some operate smoothly, others have tough times—there are also differences among stepfamilies. But comparing the two types of families on a scale of "normalcy" is like comparing apples and oranges.

183

No family type can be considered as a standard. There are no "standard" families. There are many different types of families and, using a conservative definition of a stepfamily, by the year 2000, it is estimated that there will be more stepfamilies than any other type of family in the United States. As a type of American family the stepfamily has come of age.

Children grow and develop into adults whether you want them to or not, or whether they want to or not, in whatever types of family they are in. Indeed, their growth and development are affected by the culture in which they live—whether they choose to be affected or not—and by the random events that take place in their lives. However, people's views of what happens to them, rather than the actual events, often deeply affect their feelings and behavior. So if stepfamilies consider themselves to be second-rate families, then there is the temptation to blame everything you don't like on the fact that yours is a stepfamily or that you grew up in a stepfamily!

Stepfamilies certainly are more complex than biological families and even single-parent households; however, there are many creative ways one can handle the complexities. In this book we have attempted to outline the complexities and suggest ways in which to deal with them. Often people feel that only "blood" relationships can be really deep and that the difficulties that stepparents have adjusting to their new household is due to the fact that they are not blood-related to their stepchildren and therefore the relationships can never be close—they are doomed forever. To counteract that notion, we would like to point out that during periods of war, when fathers were separated from their families for long periods of time, the fathers, upon returning, encountered the same entry problems encountered by stepparents: The children and their mother had formed a tight-knit group and discipline was not accepted from this "new" father. Lack of familiarity and not having a "place," rather than blood relatedness, make the difference—not whether the new person is a father or a stepfather. In the few cases where ex-spouses remarry after a number of years of being divorced, the reentering parent's half-grown children say, just as do stepchildren, "You can't tell me what to do! That's not the way we do it in this house!"

Another area in which individuals in stepfamilies do themselves a disservice is in forgetting that children go through various stages no matter what type of family they are in. There are patterns of child development that take place because of human factors which we all share —hormonal changes, changes in thinking patterns, emotional changes. There can be the "terrible twos" and the rebellious adolescent years regardless of the simplicity or complexity of the family structure. However, if you feel insecure about being part of a stepfamily, children pick this up quickly and use it as an explanation. For example, a frantic mother called one day saying that she and her present husband had been married for 12 years, since her son was three years old. The son, now 15, was suddenly becoming unruly and refusing to do what he was told. Although he had always had a great relationship with his stepfather, he was now saying, "You can't tell me what to do, you're not my father." The stepfather was crushed, and so was the mother, but they were willing to consider that the teenager had found a button to push and that his behavior really didn't signal any change in his basic feelings about his stepfather. It was simply his stage of development. After that, the stepfather tossed off the comment and that particular behavior stopped, though the adolescent continued to test the limits as adolescents do.

Blood relationships start "from scratch" and emotional bonding seems to take place quickly. Non-blood relationships develop more slowly and do not thrive if they are forced. But deep friendships and good marital relationships certainly illustrate the depth of love and caring possible between individuals not related by common ancestry.

One of the positive aspects of growing up in a stepfamily is the opportunity of experiencing caring and loving people who bring added dimensions to your life because of the differences between you. As one grown stepson said recently, "I don't think I would have chosen my stepbrother Tom to be my friend because we are very different. But my relationship with him has given me so much, and I value it and work on it because I want to do so. This is something very special I got from this stepfamily."

Another special thing about stepfamilies is that children have more models to use in figuring out what kind of people they want to be. Chil-

All families experience stressful times. Children tend to show little day-to-day appreciation for their parents, and at times they get angry and reject their biological parents. Because stepfamilies are families born of loss, the mixture of feelings can be even more intense than in biological families. Jealousy, rejection, guilt, and anger can be more pronounced, and therefore expectations that the stepfamily will live "happily ever after" are even more unrealistic than in first families. Having an understanding and acceptance of the many negative as well as positive feelings can result in less disappointment and more stepfamily enjoyment.

dren are not born believing you can only have one mother person and one father person, and so when they are given the opportunity to experience and enjoy, without guilt or anxiety, a number of parental figures, they experience a richness in the diversity. And even when there may have been rejection of a stepparent by stepchildren when they were younger, many, many grown stepchildren recall the warm and loving relationships they had and now have with their stepparents.

Erma Bombeck (Reader's Digest, May 1980) wrote of her rejection of all the things her stepfather did for her. After all, he wasn't her *real* father. And then, when she was grown and on her own, she suddenly realized that he was a true and loving person to her and very "real" indeed.

For some children, there have been conflicts with a biological parent and a stepparent can be a most important substitute. Often the children can love their biological parent more when they don't need to receive so much from that one person. The children often like to think of their stepparent as a very, very special friend. As one 15-year-old girl said, "I like having a stepmother because I can talk to her about things I can't tell my mother. I love them both, but my mother wouldn't be able to be objective the way my stepmother is, because she's too close to me."

The objectivity of stepparents can be most helpful if remarried parents will listen carefully without feeling insecure and threatened. Parent-child relationships and ways of doing things and interacting develop so slowly and unconsciously that sometimes unproductive patterns are not changed because the ones involved don't even know they exist. Someone new on the scene can often see the pattern just the way you can see the relationship and behavior patterns of your friends and their children. So if you and your partner have a good relationship, you may be able to give one another some very valuable feedback about ways of relating to the children. For example, one little boy, Larry, and his father had slowly developed a pattern in which the father kept doing many things for his son that Larry could now do for himself, in this way robbing the six-year-old of the sense of independence and mastery that comes with such accomplishments. Larry's stepmother was a solid support who helped him grow when she was able to indicate to her husband that a pattern had developed that was not allowing Larry the sense of independence and accomplishment he needed.

All too often marital relationships and parent-child relationships are taken for granted. There is the feeling that once the marriage vows have been said, the commitment is sealed and the relationship will remain intact and unchanging without nourishment and careful tending. It will somehow take care of itself. Then there are children and the fact of their existence is also all too often taken for granted. It is as though the children will be around forever and so working on developing a relationship can wait until the new house is completed, there is a comfortable savings account in the bank and the special television shows are over. Often a death, an affair, new job or a divorce suddenly crashes in and brings the inadequacies of the marital relationship and the parent-child relationships into sharp focus.

It may be too late to nurture and re-do the marriage relationship, but a family crisis is often the point at which parents become acutely aware of their relationship with their children. Suddenly interpersonal relationships are valued and nourished and not allowed to go untended and unnoticed. A very important lesson has been learned. By not taking human beings for granted simply because you are living together, you will no doubt find that you are talking to your partner and to the children about things that really matter. No longer are football and tennis and the weather the only topics of conversation. The result can be heightened emotional awareness of one another and a feeling of contact with other human beings which may replace the sense of isolation and loneliness you may have felt if there had been somewhat distant "cool" relationships in your previous household.

Human beings are constantly growing and changing and often couples grow apart rather than closer together as they shift in less compatible directions. With the shift in marital expectations, particularly on the part of women, many divorces have resulted. A remarriage can give you a new opportunity to develop an intimate relationship you may have always wanted. Intimate relationships are sometimes difficult to work out because the emotional closeness stirs up many feelings from very early childhood relationships. If you find you are having problems working out your new couple relationship, it is worth seeking outside help early so that you can work on finding the satisfactions you both want. In addition, seeing a couple caring about one another and working out complicated situations together is an important model for the children. Unless they were very young at the time of the divorce or parental death, they probably have experienced discord and disintegration of a couple relationship. The children in a stepfamily have an opportunity to experience and observe an example of a relationship that can renew their faith in their own future adult relationships—an invaluable gift. One young child drew a picture of his family, including parents, stepparents and step-siblings. Underneath he labeled the picture "My Super Family."

A young woman looking back on her years of growing up spoke of some of the positive and negative feelings and experiences in her stepfamily that had meant a great deal in her growth and development:

> The men I went out with always were somebody very straight, and then somebody very radical, and then somebody very straight. I think it's taken me longer to decide who I am, and who I wanted to marry. So I'm a different person and a more complicated and richer person from having different types of people in my family. I think it was more confusing putting it together, but I think it was richer. For me I think that I resented having to share, and lots of other things too, but I think that there has been so much more that is positive that I've gotten from having a stepfamily.

I've been struck this year by a sign which says something to the effect that the greatest gift a father can give to his children is to love their mother. The meaning I took from this is that the degree to which the children sense a lack of commitment between the parents, to that extent their insecurity increases. With no model of a close, effective, parent-couple bond, children will be less able to establish close marital relationships themselves in later years. I'm glad I saw Mom and my stepdad's close relationship to one another.*

Because of the added stresses in stepfamilies, it is easy to concentrate on the negatives and forget the positives. This is true for any kind of family. There are satisfactions and dissatisfactions; when you start looking for drawbacks in anything, they can certainly be found. Unfortunately, many people forget that there are very few absolutely perfect situations or perfect solutions—despite disappointments, they keep looking for them and feeling upset that their expectations are not met. There are many limitations in life, and there are many disturbing and unhappy events. These facts, however, produce the challenges of life and then the sense of satisfaction that comes from mastering these challenges.

Numerous stepfamily adults speak eloquently about the personal strength and satisfaction they feel in learning to cope successfully with this new type of family. One woman expresses her joy in her stepfamily this way:

My husband and ex-husband are best of friends and Betty (my ex-husband's wife) is also my best friend. I had four children when Joe and I got married. Betty had one child when she married Bob. They now have two more young children. Both fathers gave their daughter away (when one daughter married). The children love it.

Betty's children call me "Aunt Jane" and my children call her "Mom." Joe is called "Dad" by my children and so is their real

---

*From E. B. Visher and J. S. Visher, *Stepfamilies: A Guide to Working with Stepparents and Stepchildren.* New York: Brunner/Mazel, 1979, pp. 258-9.

Dad. Betty's children call Joe "Uncle Joe." We are very proud of this relationship even though many people do not understand or believe it. For seven years we wouldn't speak so it didn't work out for awhile. [Then] we found out the hard way that [there is] enough love to go around.

Even when stepfamilies don't work so smoothly there are many re-wards—a special card from a stepchild marking the budding of trust and caring, a toast to a stepfather at a wedding thanking him for his years of financial and emotional support, the sharing of the birth of a baby by all the parents and stepparents involved.

One stepmother put the feelings into words very well, "There is a richness and joy as well as a feeling of great accomplishment that can be achieved when one has mastered difficulty, a feeling of unity be-tween people who have shared in these endeavors, and a glow of warmth and acceptance between family or stepfamily members who have traveled this arduous journey together and have thereby proven to each other and to themselves the love and respect they feel."

Look into the mirror again and be proud of the complex family you see—different features, different skills, different ways of talking and dressing, different ways of doing things, but unified by a sense of loyalty that comes from struggling together to work out the stepfamily challenges.

In many ways, the very characteristics that make for added stresses and challenges in stepfamilies are the same ones that can offer special rewards for the members of stepfamilies. The need to deal with losses and changes can prepare your children as well as you, yourself, to meet in creative and productive ways the myriad of losses and changes throughout life. The fact that you come together from a variety of family backgrounds and traditions gives all of you the opportunity to grow and broaden your horizons as you negotiate new ways of doing things and communicate together to forge new meaningful traditions for your family. Special rituals and traditions form the basis not only of present emotional satisfactions, but also create the memories that sustain and bind individuals together for years to come.

The fact that there are new relationships to be nourished between stepparents and stepchildren, between step-siblings, and between the new couple focuses attention on the importance of interpersonal relationships. It is clear that simply being together does not provide the necessary conditions for the existence of satisfying and sustained interpersonal relationships. Relationships between people take thought and effort and are precious indeed. Members of stepfamilies are well aware of the short-lived nature of taken-for-granted personal contacts, and paying attention to making possible the growth of new relationships and preserving former parent-child relationships can produce an atmosphere of caring and emotional commitment that is very special indeed. Imagine the depth of feelings that was touched when this seventh grader's paper came home from school: *"The Person I Admire the Most.* The person I admire the most would probably be my stepfather. I admire him because he makes sure I have what I need. He buys me clothes to wear, food to eat, and a home to live in. He also gave me an education, and makes things for me such as a backboard for my tennis practice so I can play better, a chin-up bar so he and I can strengthen our muscles, and an asphalt pad that would improve my roller skating. When I need help with my school assignments he helps me the best he can. And I want to be just like him when I become a father."

Because stepchildren do have more important parenting adults in their lives and more than one household environment in which to live, there is less responsibility placed on the shoulders of any one adult. For the children, the richness and variety that results provide them with more choices in their lives. For adults and children alike, there is the opportunity for knowing individuals who of necessity are cast in a mold other than your own because of previous years of different experiences. There is an inner emotional stretching and a new understanding that come from learning to accept and value persons different from yourself.

Sometimes stepfamilies are considered "recycled" families or "second-time-around" families, and there grows a feeling that all the wonderful "first-time experiences" are in the past—a child's first step, a first meal at a particular restaurant, a first trip to Disneyworld, the renting of a first apartment. Yes, there have been these "firsts," and other "firsts" as well, for every new day brings fresh opportunities for newness—and an event or relationship never experienced before. Yes, there have been these days in the past, but there are new days now, in the present, and many more to come in the future. You may receive your first birthday card from a stepchild, listen to your child's first tears of rejection by his or her first love, or walk at dawn on a beautiful beach for the first time. Perhaps you will watch a powerful new movie with your partner, have an old-fashioned taffy-pull the day before Halloween, or experience the first emotionally satisfying and close couple relationship of your life. Every day is a new day. Unlimited possibilities stretch in front of you!

Appendix A

COMPARISON OF AMERICAN FAMILY PATTERNS

Appendix A. Comparison of American Family Patterns

Stepfamilies	First Marriage Families	Single-Parent Families	Adoptive Families	Foster Families
Family born of loss-of parent-child relationships, relationships with grandparents, dreams of what marriage and family was going to be. (Plus usual life changes).	Usual changes of living space, jobs, etc. which involve loss of familiar community.	For adults and children all are dealing with loss of important relationships, dreams, (plus usual life changes).	For older children—loss of familiar friends, school, and environment.	For children, loss of family, friends, and familiar surroundings.
All members come with past family histories	Two adults come together with past family histories.	All start with similar recent family history.	Children with different family histories join an existing group if children are not infants.	Children with a different family history join an existing group.
Parent-child bonds are older than the new couple relationship	—	—	Parent-child bonds are older than couple relationships *only* in adoption of stepchild.	—
There is a biological parent somewhere else.	—	There is a biological parent elsewhere.	There are biological parents elsewhere.	There are biological parents elsewhere.
Children often belong in two different households.	—	Children often belong in two different households.	—	Children may belong in two different households.
There is no legal relationship between the stepparent and the stepchild	—	—	—	No legal relationship between adults and foster children.

Adapted from *Stepfamilies: A Guide to Working with Stepparents and Stepchildren*, by Emily B. Visher and John S. Visher. New York: Brunner/Mazel, 1979.

Appendix B

HELPFUL BOOKS

Berman, Claire. (1982). *What Am I Doing in a Stepfamily?* New York, NY: Carol Publishing Group.

Berman, Claire. (1986). *Making It as a Stepparent: New Roles, New Rules.* New York, NY: Harper & Row.

Bernstein, Anne. (1989). *Yours, Mine, and Ours: How Families Change When Remarried Parents Have a Child Together.* New York, NY: (Scribner) Macmillan.

Brown, Laurence & Brown, Marc. (1988). *Dinosaurs Divorce: A Guide for Changing Families.* Boston, MA: Little, Brown.

Burns, Cherie. (1986). *Stepmotherhood: How to Survive Without Feeling Frustrated, Left Out or Wicked.* New York, NY: Harper & Row.

Coale, Helen. (1980). *All About Families the Second Time Around.* Atlanta, GA.: Peachtree Publishing.

Cohen, Miriam. (1989). *Long Distance Parenting: A Guide for Divorced Parents.* New York, NY: New American Library.

Diamond, Susan. (1985). *Helping Children of Divorce: A Handbook for Parents and Teachers.* New York, NY: Schocken Books.

Dodson, Fitzhugh. (1987). *How to Discipline with Love.* New York, NY: New American Library.

Evans, Marla. (1988). *This Is Me and My Two Families.* New York, NY: Magination Press.

All of these books are available at this writing from: Stepfamily Association of America, Inc., 215 Centennial Mall S., Suite 212, Lincoln, NE 68508.

Fassler, David, Lash, Michele, & Ives, Sally. (1988). *Changing Families: A Guide for Kids and Grownups.* Burlington, VT: Waterfront Books.

Getzoff, Ann & McClenahan, Carolyn. (1984). *Stepkids: A Survival Guide for Teenagers in Stepfamilies.* New York, NY: Walker & Co.

Gorman, Tony. (1985). *Stepfather.* Boulder, CO: Gentle Touch.

Isaacs, Susan. (1986). *Who's in Control? A Parent's Guide to Discipline.* New York, NY: Putnam Publishing Group.

Keshet, Jamie. (1986). *Love and Power in the Stepfamily: A Practical Guide.* New York, NY: McGraw.

LeShan, Eda. (1976). *Learning to Say Good-Bye: When a Parent Dies.* New York, NY: Macmillan.

Mala, Burt. (1989). *Stepfamilies Stepping Ahead: An Eight-Step Program for Successful Family Living.* Lincoln, NE: Stepfamily Association of America.

Newman, George. (1981). *101 Ways To Be a Long Distance Superdad.* Saratoga, CA: R & E Pubs.

Prilik, Pearl. (1990). *Stepmothering—Another Kind of Love.* New York, NY: Berkley.

Ricci, Isolina. (1980). *Mom's House, Dad's House: Making Shared Custody Work.* New York: Macmillan.

Savage, Karen & Adams, Patricia. (1988). *The Good Stepmother: A Practical Guide.* Knob Noster, MO: Crown.

Somervill, Charles. (1989). *Stepfathers: Struggles and Solutions.* Louisville, KY: Westminster John Knoy.

Vigna, Judith. (1984). *Grandma Without Me.* Niles, IL: A. Whitman.

Vigna, Judith. (1980). *She's Not My Real Mother.* Niles, IL: A. Whitman.

Wesson, Carolyn. (1988). *Teen Troubles: How To Keep Them from Becoming Tragedies.* New York, NY: Walker & Co.

Appendix C
DIAGRAMS OF POSSIBLE INTERACTIONS

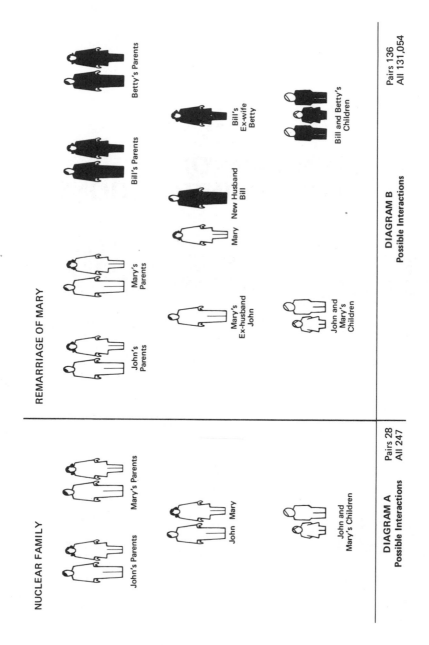

NUCLEAR FAMILY

John's Parents

Mary's Parents

John Mary

John and Mary's Children

DIAGRAM A
Possible Interactions

Pairs 28
All 247

REMARRIAGE OF MARY

John's Parents

Mary's Parents

Bill's Parents

Betty's Parents

Mary's Ex-husband John

Mary New Husband Bill

Bill's Ex-wife Betty

John and Mary's Children

Bill and Betty's Children

DIAGRAM B
Possible Interactions

Pairs 136
All 131,054

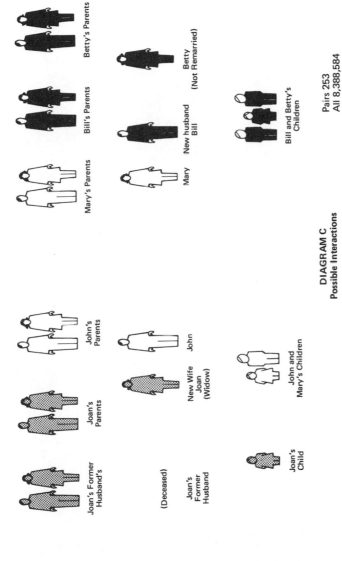

REMARRIAGE OF MARY AND JOHN

Joan's Former Husband's Parents

Joan's Parents

John's Parents

Mary's Parents

Bill's Parents

Betty's Parents

(Deceased)

Joan's Former Husband

New Wife Joan (Widow)

John

Mary

New husband Bill

Betty (Not Remarried)

Joan's Child

John and Mary's Children

Bill and Betty's Children

Pairs 253
All 8,388,584

DIAGRAM C
Possible Interactions

Diagrams A, B, and C courtesy of Carolyn McClenahan, M.S., Los Gatos, California

Index

About the Authors

Emily B. Visher, Ph.D., and John S. Visher, M.D., are founders of the Stepfamily Association of America (215 Centennial Mall S., suite 212, Lincoln, NE 68508, 402-477-STEP), an organization for stepfamilies, and authors of the widely used professional volumes *Old Loyalties, New Ties* and *Stepfamilies: A Guide to Working with Stepparents and Stepchildren*. Specialists in working therapeutically with remarried families, they are internationally known for their workshops for stepfamilies and also for mental health professionals.